INTERPRETING

FOR

INTERNATIONAL CONFERENCES

Problems of Language and Communication

DANICA SELESKOVITCH

Professor, University of Paris III, Sorbonne Nouvelle

Translated by

Stephanie Dailey
and
Eric Norman McMillan

Published by   Pen and Booth
               1608 R Street, N.W.
               Washington, D.C. 20009

Translation and adaptation of
L'interprète dans les conférences internationales –
problèmes de langage et de communication
published by Minard, Paris, 1968. Tous droits réservés.

Library of Congress No. 94-68934
ISBN 0-9605686-3-8

Printed in the United States of America.

To

Marie-France Skuncke,

who first taught me how to interpret.

TABLE OF CONTENTS

CHAPTER IV: EXPRESSION

CHAPTER V: INTERPRETING IN PRACTICE

PREFACE

by Maurice Gravier
Professor, University of Paris — Sorbonne

The conference interpreter plays a very important role in international affairs. Young people who read magazines or keep up with the latest news on television see an interpreter standing between two heads of state. It is easy to see why he is there in the middle. He helps the two VIPs overcome the language barrier and understand each other better; he helps dispel their suspicions and perhaps even makes it possible for them to reach an agreement. Interpreters are thus often involved in discussions of paramount importance to mankind which can lead to peace or war, happiness or despair, poverty or a more equitable distribution of wealth. Many young people secretly identify with this unobtrusive and knowledgeable individual who is instrumental in establishing valuable ties between the world's leaders.

This is why schools of interpretation are swamped with applicants. But can all those who wish to become interpreters qualify? What qualities do interpreters need in order to switch with lightning speed not only from one language to another, but from one conference or seminar to another and even from one mental universe to another? They must be able to move rapidly from one sphere of knowledge or human activity to another: from economics to physics, from politics to textiles or to the leather trade. To judge by the enquiries I have received and those addressed to the Secretariat of our School of Interpretation, too few people ask themselves this question, or ask it correctly. The way these enquiries are phrased proves all too clearly that the public at large has a very vague and very inaccurate picture of what interpretation is all about.

Just yesterday I answered a call in my office only to hear an innocent voice enquire, "Do you offer classes in Portuguese at your school?" to which I answered, "I'm sorry, sir, you've made a mistake. A school of interpretation is not a language teaching institution. What we teach is the technique of interpretation, and only those persons who are perfectly fluent in two foreign languages and who can handle their native tongue with eloquence and precision are admitted to the program. These aspiring interpreters must also be versatile and they must be fast thinkers. Furthermore, they must have an inborn curiosity and must have the ability to take an interest in each and every area of human activity. Lastly, interpretation requires that one have nerves of steel, great self-control and acute and sustained powers of concentration."

My unseen caller had nothing further to say, and I hung up the phone. It was then time for me to conduct a foreign visitor on a tour of the school, which also included a description of how interpreters are trained. I showed him the interpretation classrooms with their booths and simultaneous interpretation equipment. However, I also described what is involved in consecutive interpretation — perhaps the most noble of all types of interpretation — describing how an interpreter, after having listened to a speech delivered in English, and without the aid of a machine, reconstructs and delivers the speech in French, not only rendering the correct meaning but also maintaining the tone of the original, the sparkle that makes ideas come alive. A good interpreter must, of necessity, be a good public speaker capable of arousing his audience and, if need be, convincing them. In a flash of inspiration the visitor said, "Sir, I have an idea. You should teach shorthand here at your school."

No, my dear man. Shorthand has no place in a school for interpreters. The interpreter does not string words together. He does not have enough time to piece his mosaic together stone by stone. The method he uses is nothing like that of the translator. Instead, he must quickly take apart the original speech and reassemble it with a certain flair, following the bent of his own character, but particularly the character of the language into which he is interpreting.

How does he achieve this miraculous feat? I shall not attempt to explain it to you. I shall leave that to Danica Seleskovitch, who does a brilliant job of it. She is particularly qualified to do so, since she has had a long and extremely successful career in this profession. She helped found the International Association of Conference Interpreters and served as its Executive Secretary for many years. But she is also a born teacher, and her analyses will be of interest to both psychologists and guidance counselors. However, we also hope that many young students will read this clear and well thought-out book and reflect on it afterwards. It is probably not necessary to train large numbers of interpreters. However, we should seek out those young people who are most likely to succeed at this very difficult, worthy and socially important profession. Danica Seleskovitch's book will undoubtedly dispel the heady illusions of some, but it will also, I am sure, inspire many long-lasting and worthwhile careers.

CHAPTER I

INTRODUCTION

"Menschen haben Augen zum Lesen und nicht zum Sehen."

BRECHT, Galilei.

Today the barriers to communication have been all but eliminated. Airplanes which bring large cities within a few hours of one another have caused us to measure distances, not in miles or kilometers, but in hours of flying time. Radio and television bring information and ideas into the remotest of households. Societies which were unaware of each other's existence for centuries have emerged from their age-old isolation and are today in daily contact with one another. Technical innovations are put into use simultaneously in all parts of the globe, and everywhere life is becoming more and more similar.

Although science and technology have succeeded in eliminating most of the barriers that have separated men from each other, one barrier remains that runs counter to this trend, and that constitutes a hurdle which has proved well nigh insurmountable despite all the forces working to enhance human contact. This is the language barrier, the original curse, the biblical Tower of Babel.

Language, as the expression of civilizations which it helps to fashion, has so far resisted mechanization. In spite of the enormous resources invested since the last war, the translation machine does not yet do a satisfactory job. A report by the National Research Council of the United States, published in November 1966, assessed the previous ten years of research and the $19 million spent in the area by the U.S. Government alone. The report found that the human translator is 21% faster and clearer and 10% more accurate than the machine; and he is, we hasten to add, decidedly cheaper. Although the exact percentages may be debatable, the tenor of these statistics is sufficiently striking to be borne in mind.

Translators and interpreters thus have many years of work ahead of them in an area where the machine is still ineffectual. These twin professions have the same goal, act on the same principle

1

and are — or can be — based on the same theory. Yet, although the terms "translator" and "interpreter" are often used interchangeably, they do represent two rather different professions. So, before launching into the subject of this book, we should probably define the difference between them. Translation converts a written text into another written text, while interpretation converts an oral message into another oral message. This difference is crucial. In translation, the thought that is studied, analyzed and subsequently rendered in the other language is contained in a permanent setting: the written text. Good or bad, this text is static, immutable in its form and fixed in time. And the translation, equally circumscribed within a written text, is intended, as was the original, for a public the translator does not know. Conference interpreting represents something entirely different. The conference interpreter is there with both speaker and listener, dealing with messages whose fleeting words are important, not because of their form, but almost entirely because of their meaning. He participates in a dialogue, his words are aimed at a listener whom he addresses directly and in whom he seeks to elicit a reaction, and he does this at a speed that is about 30 times greater than that of the translator.

Interpretation, more limited in its goals, more instantaneous than translation, is just as old a profession. Since man has existed, and since he has used language, he has made use of intermediaries in order to communicate from one language to another. We could say that interpretation has always existed. However, in the recent past the scope of human knowledge has broadened to the point where it transcends national boundaries in every field, and it has become increasingly frustrating to have to communicate through fragmentary linguistic knowledge or ad-hoc intermediaries. This is why, with the increasing number of intellectual exchanges and the establishment of international organizations, interpretation has increasingly and quite rapidly tended to become a profession practiced by specialists.

Today there are two basic types of interpretation: consecutive interpretation and simultaneous interpretation. In consecutive the interpreter gives his interpretation after the speaker has finished his speech, which may last anywhere from a few seconds (a few dozen words) to several minutes (a few hundred or even a few thousand words).

Consecutive, formerly the sole method of interpretation, in which elders of the profession such as André Kaminker and Jean Herbert earned their reputation, is relatively infrequent nowadays. It had its heyday in the League of Nations and, until recently, in the Security Council of the United Nations. Current statistics show that less than 10% of interpretation is still done in consecutive, primarily at conferences involving two languages.

Simultaneous interpretation conveys a message into another language at virtually the same moment in time as it is expressed in the first language. The interpreter lags, at most, a few seconds behind the speaker. The speaker speaks continuously into a microphone; the sound of his voice is transmitted to the interpreter who, in turn, speaks in his own language into a microphone that transmits his words to those listening to that language. The widespread use of simultaneous interpretation began after World War II, first at the Nuremberg Trials and then at the United Nations. Broadcasts in English on an American radio network of the discussions in the General Assembly did much to establish the prestige of conference interpreters. Interpreters who rendered speeches of the Soviet delegates into English became stars of the current events scene. Since that time, interpretation has penetrated into all sectors; there are no longer any European or international organizations (EU, UNESCO, FAO, UPU, WHO, OECD, ICAO) that do not have teams of interpreters sitting in their booths with headsets and microphones. Interpretation is also employed at countless non-governmental conferences and meetings. Because of simultaneous interpretation, the number of languages used in international conferences is growing and it is no longer uncommon for meetings or conferences to use four, or even nine, working languages.

In 1953 the first conference interpreters founded a professional association.[1] This Geneva-based organization now has a membership of over 2,000 interpreters in 70 countries and six continents.

Many schools of interpretation have also sprung up since the war. Very unequal in quality, they have understood the desire of thousands of young people to be involved in current affairs while

---

[1]AIIC (International Association of Conference Interpreters), 10, Avenue de Sécheron, CH-1202 Geneva, Switzerland.

making active use of their language skills. The training that they provide is unfortunately often inadequate, given the requirements of the job. This is not surprising because the interpretation process remains somewhat arcane, and is often misunderstood. There is a tendency to see merely its linguistic side and to view it as just a kind of verbal transfer process – to use a metaphor, the interpreter is seen as a person who can convert a red shape into a blue or green one, with each color representing a different language.

To the conference delegate, interpretation thus appears to be a series of encoding and decoding operations. The message that he emits in his own code to the interpreter is converted into another code to which he does not have the key. When he speaks in German or Russian, his message is "coded" into English or French just as it would be taken down in shorthand or put into Morse code, or simply transcribed on paper. The speaker assumes that the meaning of the message is of no concern to the interpreter, since the interpreter deals solely with the form of the message. An understanding of the message is therefore felt to be unnecessary for the task at hand, which is seen as a purely mechanical operation; the interpreter need only be fully conversant with the signs belonging to each coding system he handles in order to find the correct counterpart in the other code. The interpreter is seen as a sort of automaton whose codes are his working languages, and the signs comprising these codes are words. The delegate assumes that as soon as the interpreter hears a given word, he automatically – through extensive practice – finds its equivalent in the other language.

But is this what really happens? Do the interpreters of the United Nations, UNESCO, the EU, and at countless private meetings and conferences perform the mechanical operation described above? We shall see that, for reasons inherent in the very nature of language, the interpreter could never operate in this manner and that the mental processes involved in interpretation are entirely different.

That is why, before analyzing this process, we would like the reader to have a more realistic idea of what is involved in interpretation by divorcing it from the multilingual, language-juggling aspects of the exercise.

Imagine a situation where two people are speaking to each other in the same language but are separated by a soundproof glass wall. They can see each other but they cannot hear each other (in the same way that speakers of different languages cannot "hear" each other). They can speak to each other through two intermediaries placed on either side of the glass wall. These intermediaries are the only ones capable of hearing both speakers and it is their job to transmit what is said on one side of the wall to the person on the other side. We can imagine what would happen: the speakers on either side of the wall would see each other and talk to each other without addressing themselves directly to either of the intermediaries, whose only role here would be to overcome the acoustical barrier. Each speaker would stop talking at certain points to allow enough time for the intermediary to repeat what he had just said. The speaker would stop speaking after expressing a complete idea, let us say after every three minutes. One minute of sustained speech corresponds to an average of 150 words, and at the end of three minutes one speaker would have uttered 450 words. It is obvious that the intermediary would be incapable of repeating, *word for word*, statements of that length that he had heard only once. But will he be able to do what he is supposed to, namely transmit the meaning of what has been said, the semantic content of the speech? Well, each one of us can relate the plot of a book we have just read, even though it may contain some tens of thousands of words. Why, then, shouldn't it be possible to repeat what was stated in a message containing 400 or 500 words? The reader will agree, however, that in order to do this, the intermediary must have *understood* what he heard (because if not, the rendering of the *message* will be incoherent or incorrect). This means that one must not only *know the language of the speakers* but also something about the *topic* being discussed.

The same principle applies in *consecutive interpretation*. If the interpreter *is fluent in the two languages* involved, conversant with the *subject matter* and, through a very rigorous analysis, grasps the meaning of what is said, he can restate the message. We will see that, once he has understood the meaning behind the speaker's words, he is capable of rendering the original message in its entirety.

The process involved in *simultaneous interpretation* can be compared to the radio broadcast of a soccer game. The sportscaster, who describes for his listeners the action that is unfolding before his very eyes, analyzes very rapidly and accurately the events which the listeners cannot see and transmits them to the listeners in their own language. Unlike the Morse-code operator, he does not encode a set of symbols into another set of symbols, but rather analyzes and explains the meaning of the events taking place; he is in no way thrown off balance by the need to describe one form of expression (the action of the players on the field) in terms of another (the play-by-play verbalization of that action). The simultaneous interpreter analyzes the statements that he receives through the medium of language in like manner. He does not concentrate solely on the language, any more than he ponders over the expressions he will use to express himself in the other language; rather, he carries out a rapid analysis and spontaneously states what has been said, thereby transmitting the semantic content of the message. And if this semantic content that he conveys is the same as the original, his rendition of the message will — as we shall see — necessarily reflect the style of the original.

But is it possible for an interpreter who has had no technical training to convey the semantic content of highly technical messages? Of course not. It is impossible to understand a message without having some knowledge of the subject being discussed. But the problem is not as straightforward as people are wont to believe. The interpreter is not faced with the choice of being either a specialist in the subject matter or simply repeating what he hears, word for word, in another language. Both alternatives are equally impossible. Throughout this book we shall describe the type of knowledge that an interpreter must have and the way in which that knowledge makes comprehension possible.

We shall also see that interpretation invalidates the naive theory about languages which was held to be true for centuries, but which has been disproven by the findings of modern linguistics. This theory held that each word in a language is a symbol and that it has a semantic "twin" in every other language which is identical to it and can serve as a ready translation of it in any context.

This is patently untrue. Unlike numbers, which have identical equivalents in other languages but are articulated differently in each language, words evoke a semantic field which is infinitely more vast than their immediate meaning and do not have absolute equivalents in other languages. If it were possible, as so many delegates at international conferences still tend to believe, merely to "repeat" the individual words of one language in a foreign language, simultaneous

6

interpretation would be child's play. But words being, as they are, open to an infinity of meanings contingent upon context, situation, audience, etc., a word-for-word translation would only render the primary meaning of the word; the message would not come through clearly and would be little short of incomprehensible. Even if you were to attempt this exercise, you would quickly see the practical impossibility of performing it, given the speed at which it must be carried out. Only words that have similar etymologies and similar phonology can be reproduced at this speed. If you are not convinced of this, try it yourself. Ask a friend to take an encyclopedia in a foreign language that you know well and to select at random about four or five hundred words. Then have the friend, timer in hand, read these words to you in three minutes, i.e., at normal speaking speed. As your friend is speaking, try to "repeat" those same words in English. You will see right away that you cannot spontaneously retrieve words that you know unless some logical thought process brings them to the fore.

We are now beginning to see what interpretation entails. It is not the oral translation of words — rather, it uncovers a meaning and makes it explicit for others. It is a process of exegesis and explanation. Interpreters are, in this way, no different from musicians or actors who transform the writings of a composer or a poet while nevertheless meticulously preserving the message; the greater their interpreting talent, the more comprehensible the message becomes.

But what about language? Can a definition of conference interpreting exclude language and linguistic problems? Definitely not. If we seem to be playing down the linguistic side of the problem, this is to prevent it from eclipsing more important aspects of interpretation. Language does give rise to some difficulties, but they are in addition to the compelling problems of analysis and elucidation.

Interpretation is communication, i.e., analysis of the original message and its conversion into a form accessible to the listener. The means of communication — languages — are working tools, but by no means the final goal. Thus the interpreter is not a linguist who studies a specific aspect of language; rather he possesses a full and intuitive knowledge of the languages that he uses in the practice of his profession. These languages are the means by which the interpreter enables the listener to understand the message addressed to him. He does so through a process that obtains for both consecutive and simultaneous interpretation.

The process, broken down into its three stages, is roughly as follows:

1. Auditory perception of a linguistic utterance which carries meaning. Apprehension of the language and comprehension of the message through a process of analysis and exegesis;

2. Immediate and deliberate discarding of the wording and retention of the mental representation of the message (concepts, ideas, etc.);

3. Production of a new utterance in the target language which must meet a dual requirement: it must express the original message in its entirety, and it must be geared to the recipient.

It is not the purpose of this book to describe the specific techniques employed by interpreters in consecutive and simultaneous interpretation. It is, rather, to shed light on the mental processes that make possible the virtually instantaneous transmission of an oral message into another language. We have briefly described the basic problems that confront a person who must transmit in "real time" a message which was not intended for him. There are problems of comprehension, problems of knowledge, problems of communication and also problems of language.

At first glance, these problems seem almost insurmountable to one who is not a specialist in the field. The first interpreters who overcame these problems with seeming ease were viewed as linguistic geniuses and masters of verbal dexterity. Today these problems are overcome every day by hundreds of conference interpreters throughout the world, proving that interpretation *is* possible. We propose to examine the techniques and mental processes that enable the conference interpreter to successfully play the role of intermediary.

It goes without saying that, in the actual practice of interpretation, the intellectual steps that we will examine here one by one do not occur in succession but actually overlap, and the relative weight of each component in the overall process depends on the type of message involved. In describing this process, we have attempted to explain the demands put on the interpreter and the responses required, which often approach the limits of human endurance. Most often, the interpreter manages to meet the challenge because of his talent and mastery of technique.

We also felt it would be helpful if we chose not to limit our study to the *interpretive process* alone, but to add a chapter on *interpreting at conferences*. Many have heard about the United Nations and its interpreters in their glass booths. Some may want to become interpreters themselves or to explore problems of communication. As civilizations grow and seek closer links with each other – a United Europe, the English-speaking world, the Arab world, the Chinese world – vast new horizons unfold for the profession. Substantial problems still need to be overcome, however, before the interpreting profession can truly come into its own.

CHAPTER II

UNDERSTANDING

1. THE SPOKEN LANGUAGE

To interpret one must first understand. In this chapter we shall attempt to define what understanding is and describe in particular the type of language used at international conferences. We shall also look at the kinds of messages that are exchanged between speakers as well as the methods used by interpreters to analyze those messages.

The message that the interpreter receives and that he must understand in order to be able to reconstruct it in the other language is transmitted in an oral and spontaneous[1] form which we shall term "the spoken language."

Although practically the sole means of communication in ancient times, the spoken language later found itself — with the advent of printing and the spread of literacy — largely confined to use within the family and among close friends. At a time when travel was not as easy as it is today, books were often the first foreign travelers. It is, therefore, not surprising that foreign languages were known mostly in their written form, or that the first crossover from one language to another was done on paper, i.e., by way of the written word. The translation exercises done daily in our schools and colleges are living testimony to the primacy of the written word and to the lack of contact with the living environment out of which language springs. It is not unusual for students to spend hours during an examination translating fifteen lines which are static, frozen in time, and taken out of context.

With the advent of the telephone, radio and television, the spoken language has today regained its importance and now matches that of the written word. The spoken language is an essential tool of communication, and yet it is still treated as a stepchild — were it not

---

[1]In Chapter V.5 we shall study the special case of a prepared speech read to a conference.

for phonetics it would hardly be studied at all. Most people think that written language is all there is to language. We even tend to think of the "spoken" language as the articulation of the written language, without taking into account the special characteristics of the spoken word. Nevertheless, certain signs seem to indicate a growing awareness of the difference between the two forms of language (for example, whereas in the past a radio announcer always read from a text, today he frequently improvises). We should explore the spoken language more thoroughly, since it is of paramount importance for interpretation.

Before we speak we know what we are going to say, but until we open our mouths we do not know exactly how we are going to say it. The words we choose to convey what we mean will depend not only on us but also on the person we are addressing and the context in which we both find ourselves. This spontaneous aspect of linguistic expression allows us to concentrate on the meaning of what we intend to say and to let the choice of words and tone more or less take care of themselves. By knowing what we want to say we can utter the words "It's raining" in a matter-of-fact way, regretfully, questioningly or joyfully, but at no time do we consciously modulate our voices. By knowing what we want to say, we can formulate the most complex thoughts, and the words are immediately at our disposal. The inflection and volume of our voice, our facial expressions, our gestures, our faster or slower delivery, etc. are also spontaneous. Each of us, then, is an actor without being aware of it, and a great one, since in speaking spontaneously, we perform perfectly.

If, on the other hand, we were to stop concentrating on the meaning of what we were saying and focus our attention on its form, we would very probably stumble and be misunderstood. By the same token, this spontaneity of expression, this subordination of form to meaning, disappears if expression is dissociated in time from verbal utterance, as for example when one reads a text prepared beforehand. Every actor must incorporate gestures, facial expressions, inflection and emphasis into his art to breathe life into the playwright's work. Stanislavsky used to require his students to say "Good evening" in dozens of different ways, using a different intonation each time to reflect a different situation. We all do this unconsciously in our daily lives, varying our intonation according to the desired meaning.

Spontaneous speech goes several steps beyond this in order to convey its meaning. It functions almost cybernetically; the voice is raised to correspond to the hearing range of the listener, information that might be unknown to the listener is given more slowly and distinctly, examples are enumerated more rapidly, etc.

Lastly, spontaneous speech helps one to think. It must be remembered that although a person knows what he is going to say before he says it, his notion of it is not yet precise. A speaker does not choose his words and expressions beforehand, but once they are uttered, they shape the thoughts and serve as a kind of feedback to which the mind reacts by continuing to shape and develop the thought, so that one thinks better while one is speaking than when the thought has not yet been formulated.

The act of speaking spontaneously is thus above all the thought process at work. Thought triggers speech and the tone of voice and simultaneously reacts to them as well as to the listeners, i.e., their smiles or the movement of their heads, the approval or disapproval they exhibit. Thus the initial complete thought is fragmented by the speaker as he expresses himself, and as he adjusts his expression to the audience.

Its spontaneity and its subordination to meaning make the spoken word eminently intelligible. Let us compare it, for a moment, to the written word. It would take dozens of lines or even pages to express the meaning of one unarticulated sound or gesture. The person reading the description of such an unarticulated sound or gesture will have to carefully analyze this description in order to understand what is spontaneously grasped by the person to whom the sound or gesture is addressed. If a written text is to be read out and its meaning properly conveyed, it must be not only well written but also well presented. Yet to be understood in normal speech, all you have to think about is what you are saying.

While subordinated to meaning, the spoken language also transmits this meaning. It reflects not only the speaker's thoughts but also his thought process. It shapes the meaning more precisely and transmits this through hesitation, repetition, and association of ideas, all of which bring out the thought and unequivocally reveal its progression.

In interpretation it becomes obvious that the intelligibility of a verbal message depends on the way in which it is expressed. The speeches given at technical or scientific conferences by graduates fresh out of college are, with some rare exceptions, the most difficult to understand. Recently acquired knowledge is often merely a parroting of that developed by others. Quotation can become more important than logic, and the sequencing of ideas is not always coherent.

Evanescence

Since instant understanding is necessary, the spoken language contains − in addition to words − many elements that aid understanding: gestures, facial expressions, style of delivery, changes in volume, pauses, etc. The spoken language does not have the advantage that a written text provides of allowing a reader to review what he has just read. The content of the message must be understood at the very moment it is uttered; if not, it will vanish without trace − it will be as if it had never been uttered.

Every aspect of the spoken language is geared to meet this need. The speed of delivery is a function of the listening capacity of the listener, and the semantic density is a function of the listener's level of comprehension. These elements will vary to the extent that the information conveyed is new to the listener.

This need to be intelligible is one of the most striking aspects of the spoken language. In a dialogue where each of the speakers uses language to evoke a response from the other, the primary goal of language is always the same: to convey a message, to make oneself understood. Yet the form of expression will vary according to the person being addressed, i.e., the amount of background information the listener possesses on the subject.

We could consider every message as a point on a vast semantic field, and the language used to convey this message expands or contracts according to the listener's familiarity with the subject. For example, if in a family situation someone said, "The plumber's just left," it would be an extended form of "He's just left," but would be a more concise way of saying "The workman who unclogged the sink has just left." The message is the same, but the amount of information furnished spontaneously depends on how much the listener already knows about the situation, and thus determines the intelligibility of the message. One can imagine how many books it would take to convey this information to a Martian; one would have to start with a definition of man and social relationships and include numerous treatises on the nature of water flow. Conversely, a "Yes," or even a nod of the head, would be sufficient if the information were given in response to a question. Thus, one person could understand in one word what for another would require endless explanation. Let us consider an extreme case: proper names. When someone hears the name of a person whom he does not know, the most he can determine about that individual with a reasonable degree of probability, based on the sound of the name, will be his or her sex and national origin. Yet, to listeners who know that individual, that name could mean everything.

Thus, the information presented and the form in which it is conveyed cannot be equated. The spoken language expands and contracts according to the background of the listener: it aims to convey the message and make it understood, by saying enough without repeating what is already common knowledge to both. Any speaker has the inherent ability to adjust to his listener. Of course, the degree to which this ability is developed varies, but the linguistic adjustment is always made in the interests of communication.

Returning to the subject of international conferences, let us imagine that we have just delivered a brief, three-minute speech. We would be incapable of repeating those four or five hundred words verbatim with the original gestures and intonations, even if we were asked to do so immediately afterwards. More often than not, we would not even know what words or gestures we had used, and neither would our listeners. What sticks in our minds is the meaning, clear and precise because it was spoken aloud, but already largely amorphous in memory. Most of the words that were uttered and all of the sounds that shaped the tone of the statement are blotted out in the memories of both speaker and listener, and only the meaning that they conveyed lingers on.

Thus both speaker and listener know "what" was said. When auditory perception is compared to the visual perception of a written text, which by its very nature provides a chance for review and thereby allows the words as well as the meaning to remain, we find that auditory perception has a special quality that enables it to separate meaning from wording, and thus retain meaning and forget wording. This gives the interpreter an advantage, for in interpretation his attention is focused on meaning and is not distracted by words. Whether one likes it or not, the wording only makes a fleeting impression and, because of this, meaning and wording are automatically separated.

Since the spoken language strives at all times to make the semantic content of the message intelligible, it is obvious that the interpreter must understand the meaning of the message. Let us look once again at the example we gave in the Introduction, explaining simultaneous interpretation. It is clear that, if one needed to express a gesture through words, it would be better to explain the meaning of the gesture than to describe its kinetic aspects. When you see someone gesturing on a beach, it is easier to say "Paul's calling us" than to describe first what the man looks like, and then each of his gestures. But one might object by saying that a gesture is not language and that switching from one language to another is not nearly as drastic as switching from one code of communication to another. "Why do you have to understand to interpret?" some skeptics ask. "Why can't you simply translate what you hear?" This is a mistake that is often made because we are too accustomed to the written word.[2] We have just seen that immediate comprehension is the aim of the spoken language and that the message it transmits will never take shape unless it is understood immediately. We might add that the spoken word disappears as soon as the message is understood, and that, therefore, unlike its written counterpart which comes into being as soon as it is set to paper, the spoken message is kept alive only in the mind of the listener, who remembers the meaning it conveyed and not its form (words, gestures, intonation, etc.).

The interpreter discovers that attempts to recall the words that were uttered are of little help to him because he would also have to remember the accompanying gestures, sign language and tone of voice – in short, all the features of the spoken language. He would turn into a gesticulating clown, and by concentrating on words and facial expressions would end up speaking the target language in a

---

[2] It is worth pointing out here that translation likewise involves more than a simple word-for-word transfer.

16

way that would be totally devoid of meaning. On the other hand, by taking advantage of the qualities of the spoken language to aid his own understanding and also his expression in the target language, the interpreter not only understands the meaning of the message but refuses to let himself be hypnotized by the words, as would readily happen if he had a written text before him, which he could reread as often as he wished. Caught up in the cross-currents of ideas which meet and interconnect, the interpreter deals with people and not books. He benefits from circumstances that allow him to perform better than if he had a written text in front of him. As a matter of fact, it is an advantage for an interpreter who is experienced in analysis of meaning *to hear the speaker's words only once.* Words are actually a hindrance and not a help when one attempts to make sense out of a string of hundreds, if not thousands, of words. Taken in isolation, a word has a tendency to evoke all its current connotations and even its etymological meaning. The more evanescent, the more fleeting a word is, the easier it will be for the interpreter to discard it and retain only the meaning of the message; an accurate interpreter preserves meaning, not words.

We would, then, respond to the familiar maxim *traduttore — traditore*[3] by *scripta manent — verba volant*[4] with *verba volant* having a positive connotation, and we would emphasize *verba* because, although the speaker's *wording* may be evanescent, his *meaning* is not and is reproduced completely intact.

We are aware that, in spite of the argument we have put forth, the interpreter who is unwilling to repeat the pattern of the original words is laying himself open to the charge of having inaccurately rendered what was said. But let us not forget the situation in which the interpreter finds himself. The speaker does not know whether the interpreter has repeated what he said or not, but he can determine, by the audience's reaction, whether he has been understood or misunderstood. At a conference someone will invariably say, "That's exactly what I meant," or "I didn't explain myself clearly."

---

[3]Italian aphorism punning on the words "translator" and "traitor."

[4]Latin proverb signifying that written words (*scripta*) remain for posterity, while spoken words (*verba*) vanish.

Yet a speaker rarely tries to check on the "translation" of a single *word*. When consecutive interpretation is used there are always some people present, often including the speaker himself, who understand both the source language and the target language. The accuracy with which the meaning is conveyed and the clarity with which it is expressed lead them to think that the interpretation is correct; but they think that the reason why it is correct and complete is because it is totally literal. How can they be expected to do otherwise, given that they were raised in the tradition of the written language and the written word?

Interpretation is more like painting than photography. Photography captures every detail and perfectly reproduces all that falls within the range of the camera's lens. When compared to painting, photography often betrays what it reproduces because it reproduces indiscriminately, capturing what is of greater interest along with what is of lesser interest, the extraneous along with the essential. Translated into terms of our profession, it is as if photography reproduced words without attempting to explain their meaning. Painting, on the other hand, seeks to discover a meaning, to convey a message and, of course, reflects the object as seen through the eyes of the painter. Just as painting is not copying, interpretation is not a word-for-word translation. Perhaps one day translating machines will function as interpretation or translation cameras, but they will never reach the point where they can re-express the total message as interpreters and translators do. Just as photography will never replace painting, although it can become an instrument of creativity in the hands of an artist, machines may in the future be able to assist translators and interpreters, provided the latter direct the machine's work and human intervention is not eliminated.

The Inscrutability of Language

Intelligibility, which is the goal of the spoken language, is not merely expressed by a greater or lesser degree of explicitness − it takes other forms as well. One speaks louder to a deaf person and gestures to a person who is too far away to hear; in short, one uses the language that the other person can understand. Hence the custom — ridiculous though the outcome may be — of speaking baby talk to children or pidgin English to foreigners.

This behavioral trait reveals two things: that there is a basic desire to be understood, and at the same time that language is unable to adjust to a listener outside of normal range. If the language used with foreigners is sometimes inappropriate (one speaks too loud, as if their lack of understanding were due to a hearing disorder) it is because too many things are unknown. The speaker's desire to accommodate, to adjust to the situation, leads him into error. In international conferences, participants are more generally aware of the nature of "foreignness," but it is still more than just a question of language. And yet, speakers at international conferences speak more or less as they would if they were all nationals of the same country. Indeed, this tendency is strengthened by the presence of fellow countrymen. Foreign listeners thus receive a message in a language that is not only foreign to their ears but ill-adapted to their frame of reference. A case in point are the French, who, years after the 1960 monetary reform, continued to express amounts of money in old francs, not realizing that such figures are meaningless to foreign listeners.

This unadapted language which is often used among speakers of different nationalities could be compared to the often unintelligible snatches of conversation that one overhears on the bus or subway. Everyone must at some time have found himself at a dinner party or a reception where he was the only one who did not know all the other guests. The isolation you feel is due not only to ignorance of the topics being discussed but also to the fact that the language being used contains a number of statements that presume familiarity with the subject. People who work together in the same office or are a part of the same family possess a common background that allows them to understand one another even when they use elliptical expressions and imprecise terms. Words like "thingamabob" or "whatchamacallit" are used because they have an immediate meaning for the speaker and the listener.

Once when I was in Tunis I heard a colleague say that her route to work took her past Cairo. Since Cairo is 3,000 kilometers from Tunis anyone who was not acquainted with this person would have concluded either that she must be slightly confused or alternatively that the sentence, as spoken, was not to be taken literally; the listener would then have to try to find an internal logic in the message that would make it possible to find the key to its meaning. And, as it turned out, those present all understood that here "Cairo" meant a certain intersection on the outskirts of Tunis where there was a sign pointing the way to Cairo. An uninformed observer might have discovered the meaning of the message after thorough analysis, but it would have taken him longer to see the light than it did those familiar with the situation.

In practicing his profession, the interpreter often finds himself in the position of the uninformed observer for whom the word "Cairo" is meaningless. Suppose the phrase given above had to be interpreted into another language. If the hypothetical interpreter were to translate it word for word without analyzing it, he would end up with a faithful translation of the words but with a totally distorted meaning. Yet meaning is what counts.

The conference interpreter finds himself in the peculiar position of being neither an active listener who hears a message in a language that has been more or less tailored to his needs, nor a casual listener who does not find it necessary to understand everything completely. The speakers do not address the interpreter but rather their colleagues, who are familiar with the subject matter and context and are thus capable of understanding elliptical expressions.

Interpreters often find university professors and lawyers a joy to interpret. They are accustomed to speaking in public, to giving explanations, and are capable of formulating their thoughts in a precise manner that makes them immediately understandable. They relieve the interpreter of a good part of the burden of analyzing. But such speakers are rare.

Generally, when an interpreter is faced with the task of transmitting a message he must first understand what the speaker meant in the context and reconstitute what was implicit in the speaker's remarks, since it is unnecessary for the speaker to state what is obvious to his listeners. Next, the interpreter has to render the message intelligibly into the target language.

The interpreter is not the prime target of the message and the message is delivered in a form that is not tailored to him. All questions of linguistic knowledge aside, the interpreter will grasp the message better than the foreign participant for whom the culture of the speaker is as unknown as his language. The interpreter can clarify the underlying assumptions and, by concentrating and analyzing, can compensate for the degree of inscrutability involved.

This wall of linguistic inscrutability is especially apparent at the beginning of a meeting or during a very short conference where an interpreter is working for the first time. Afterwards, it soon disappears. But the interpreter who must start in cold at a meeting about which he knows nothing and which is already in progress is very much at a disadvantage. The meaning of the simplest message may escape him because he lacks those tools that are indispensable for analyzing it. He has no knowledge of the context, but he acquires it soon enough.

Inscrutable in its structure for the foreign listener, the message is also somewhat inscrutable for the interpreter. If he translated the message word for word, if this were possible, he would translate the language but his formulation would leave the thought inscrutable. It is precisely because he understands not only the speaker's language, but also the message being conveyed, that the interpreter is able to restate it in the target language, adapting it to the listener's capacity of comprehension. We shall return to this point in the section entitled "Expression."

To say that language is inscrutable tells us nothing about the real difficulty of the content of the message. One must uncover what is implied, yet the underlying assumptions may be quite elementary. Interpreters are always impressed by their colleagues whom they hear at meetings at which they themselves are not working. They do not always realize that, for the casual listener, the spoken language is almost always inscrutable and that the message which he does not fully understand does not necessarily conceal any special difficulties.

Since he is aware of this inscrutability of language, the interpreter becomes an exegete and his habit of analyzing helps him to uncover not only the elementary assumptions but also to understand the technical side of the issue. One day at a meeting of the International Organization for Standardization (ISO) I noted the following discussion about high-alloy steels. "What is the cooling time of this grade?" and the answer: "It's air cooled." At first glance it would seem that the response did not fit the question. However, the entire context as well as the statements that preceded this question indicated that steels to be quenched are dipped in oil, in water or in brine, depending on the degree of hardness desired. If they are cooled in air, they are self-hardening and the cooling time is normal. This example demonstrates how the simplest words can appear inscrutable if taken out of context.

Understanding inscrutable language does not pose any insurmountable problems unless one fails to understand the nature of its inscrutability. The interpreter knows that the technical jargon that he hears is not as immediately intelligible to him as it is to participants listening to the original. Yet he must transmit the message in a way that is as intelligible for his listeners as it was to those who heard it first hand. He thus sets out to analyze the message and to put it into its logical framework. He discovers the constituent parts of the message, so that broader knowledge of the context will expand his semantic range and thus enable him to interpret.

2. THE MESSAGE

What are the various features that characterize the verbal message the interpreter hears?

The Speaker

The message is naturally conditioned by the person who originates it. This person, whom we shall henceforth call "the speaker," does not necessarily possess the oratorical gifts of a Demosthenes. Anyone can take the floor at an international conference. His purpose is not to practice oratory but to communicate with foreign colleagues on an issue common to them all.

This conference speaker is also a listener, a participant. He does not express himself in the same way as a lecturer or a journalist whose intended audience is a vaguely defined public. He faces the people whom he addresses and his ideas are a reaction to the preceding statements and will themselves stimulate further comment. His "message," to use the language of communication, has an immediate purpose: to explain a thesis, defend an interest, or convince the undecided. The interpreter interprets in context, not in a vacuum; he knows that the speaker has come to the meeting with a definite purpose and that, sometimes despite all appearances, his speech has an internal coherence. He is also aware that the speaker knows more about his own field than he does.

The position a person holds, the political point of view he supports and the profession he practices will determine how he will act at a meeting. It goes without saying that the meaning of the message will vary according to whether the speaker is an importer or an exporter, a producer or a consumer, a Frenchman or a Belgian. Obviously a railroad executive would not support highway transportation unless such services were part of his own organization. The interpreter must, therefore, always know something about the speaker because his background may give a clue to the meaning of his message. When, during a conference on dams, an engineer states, with respect to a certain dam, that "the safety factor has been reduced 50%," this cannot mean that the dam is not sturdy enough, but must imply that progress has been made in building techniques. The interpreter does not know what this progress consists of — whether it is due to increased durability of the materials or to improved cross-section design. However, since he knows that the speaker is an authority on the subject he immediately recognizes the positive tone of the statement. If, however, a journalist were to say the same thing in another context, there is a strong possibility that he would mean the dam was dangerous and that there is a high probability of a disaster occurring. A statement is thus bound to be ambiguous if the listener has no information about the person who uttered it.

In order to immediately grasp the purpose of the speech and to understand its significance, the interpreter must be constantly aware of the capacity in which the person is speaking. If he persists in seeing things from his own point of view he might misunderstand what is being said. We remember one interpretation student who completely distorted the meaning of a speech because she failed to "identify" the speaker correctly. An American officer was discussing American military hospitals at the time of the Korean War; he described how the wounded were cared for and concluded by saying that the special care they received allowed them to return quickly *to the front*. At the end of a long rendition in consecutive, the student translated this final statement by saying they would "*rapidly return to their families*." The student had put herself in the position of a civilian wife or mother. Since in consecutive interpretation one jots down ideas that one has understood and not the words one has heard, it was obvious that here the interpreter had misunderstood what was said. Expecting a conclusion that would conform to her own line of reasoning, she had substituted her own thoughts for those of the speaker without "hearing" what the speaker had said.

Being mistaken about the speaker can thus seriously impair one's understanding of an entire speech. The argument takes on an unusual slant; the interpreter cannot remain detached from the speaker's words; he has the impression of having misunderstood what was said, and the interpretation rapidly deteriorates into an unintelligible literal translation.

A number of years ago I was called, on the spur of the moment, to interpret for a speaker whose name and nationality I did not know at a meeting of the Consultative Assembly of the Council of Europe. The speaker spoke the most perfect English, sprinkling his statements with the "ers" that are so characteristic of the British. Furthermore, he exhibited a cultured false modesty and had begun his speech with an anecdote, as is the custom with English speakers. I was convinced that he was English and, by the way he spoke, probably a Conservative, and I was at a loss to understand his strong appeal for a European agricultural free trade area. After botching his speech, taking the bite out of it and skirting all the ambiguities, I learned that this gentleman was Danish, and then I understood, but too late...

The reader is probably wondering why I found it necessary to tone down the speech and avoid the ambiguities instead of simply "repeating" what the gentleman said. I would refer the reader back to what I said earlier. A quick glance is sufficient to "see Paul" on the beach, but let us imagine that an animal were to pass under our very noses so quickly that we could not identify it. If we had not "understood" what we had seen, would we be capable of describing the animal so that our listeners could recognize it even though we had not recognized it ourselves? You might say that visual perception involves a synthesis but that in this case I had received my information aurally, and the Danish gentleman had provided me with enough details to allow me to reproduce the speech in spite of not having grasped the underlying meaning. I would reply that after a rapid oral delivery one remembers not the exact wording of a two or three minute passage, but only the meaning. If that is not retained, there is almost nothing left to rely on, and the interpreter who has not understood is as incapable of saying anything meaningful as the person who sees something move and, not knowing whether he has seen a snake or a mouse, will refrain from stating definitely whether he has seen one or the other. The interpreter, in an analogous situation, can only render approximate meaning and has to tone down what might be too strong.

The Inner Logic of Speech

To verify the accuracy of his understanding, the interpreter tries to relate what he has understood to what he knows about the speaker. We have seen that the capacity in which a speaker speaks has an effect on what he says. Another equally important method of verification is that of psychological likelihood. There are certain things that no one would say. The interpreter bears this fact in mind and interprets accordingly; he does not linger over the speaker's unconscious motivations, despite the reactions that they may provoke in him.

Incidentally, in daily life we all find ourselves in situations where we fail to hear something that has been said to us, either because we are too far away, or because a car passes by, etc. Problems of this type occur only too frequently in interpretation; the acoustics may be bad, the interpretation equipment may be poor, or a microphone may not be properly plugged in. This is just one more problem that the interpreter must attempt to solve while simultaneously struggling to maintain the internal coherence of the message, even if he is not certain he has heard everything correctly.

Unlike the speaker, who takes his listener more or less consciously into account, and adjusts his speech accordingly, the interpreter is a messenger. He does not solicit a direct response and does not have to respond to the reaction elicited by the message he transmits. Consequently, he scarcely needs to take a professional interest in the personalities of the people whom he interprets, except to represent them accurately through their message.

In this connection, it should be noted that, in general, the interpreter is aware that the speaker knows more about the subject matter than he does, and he finds that knowing this helps to guide him in his attempt to understand. What at first glance seems incomprehensible must, nevertheless, hold some meaning; thus the interpreter refuses to adopt the attitude of the schoolboy who, faced with the problem of a Latin translation, fails to reflect sufficiently on it and writes down what he knows is nonsense. The interpreter pursues his analysis of the message until it becomes coherent.

I remember a conference on economics where it had been stated that poor people have a greater propensity to spend than rich people. For whatever reason, the logic of this idea had escaped me and I saw in it a contradiction which I, however, refused to accept. Knowing that participants at international conferences are usually knowledgeable about their subject and that it was unlikely that the speaker had said something absurd, I refused to take the line of least resistance which would have meant shrugging it off and "repeating" a stupid statement. I looked at the problem realistically, the idea of relativity dawned on me, and although I had initially heard wrong or misunderstood, I succeeded through a process of reasoning in reconstructing the meaning of the idea.

Purpose of the Message

In international meetings the message functions cybernetically, not only because it uses language intended to drive its point home, but also because it seeks to elicit a reaction from the listener. It would be foolish to say something that had no purpose. To tell someone, out of context, "That's a big tree" could only provoke questions, starting with "Why did you say that?" To say the same thing to a worker laden with saws and ropes standing in front of a tree that has to be cut down, would be to convey a meaningful message full of implications that would gradually become explicit as more is said or after several comments have been exchanged. To understand the message, one must first understand the purpose. Once this is accomplished the interpreter is equipped with a powerful tool for analyzing the entire message.

The interpreter thus has a keen interest in the object of a speech. Let us cite one example. Advertisements for Renault say that, over a distance of 100 kilometers and at a speed of 60 km an hour, the Renault 5 will consume 4.9 liters of gasoline. One can expect that a manufacturer of automobiles will speak well of his particular model in his advertisements and that he will emphasize one of its more attractive features in order to boost sales. An interpreter who knows nothing about the way an automobile engine works and who has never heard of the relationship between speed and fuel consumption, yet who is aware of the objective of advertising, would understand that a gasoline consumption of 4.9 liters for 100 km is low in comparison with other automobiles. Yet the very fact that the figure was indicated so precisely shows that the Renault 5's consumption is not really all that much lower at speeds other than 60 km per hour, and that it changes when the speed is increased or decreased.

Determining the purpose of the speech is thus an important factor in understanding the total message, for if the purpose is not known the meaning of the entire message will be lost. Another example would involve that of opposing sides of an arbitration where both sides argue in ways that will favor their respective cases. If the uninformed observer who hears the long tirades or very detailed technical explanations is unaware of the purpose behind the statements (receiving compensation or avoiding fines) he will not be able to grasp the underlying meaning of the message and will miss the point.

Merely stating the purpose is sometimes enough to transmit the message. In consecutive interpretation, when the chairman of a meeting asks the interpreter to condense his translation, the interpreter could often accomplish this, at the risk of vexing the original speaker, by summing up a long statement with "X agrees."

I remember how surprised a member of the Board of Directors of a Franco-German consortium was when, at a meeting on mining, he ran into an interpreter whom he had often seen at meetings involving politicians or electrical engineers. He could not understand how it was possible for an interpreter to perform with the same skill in such different areas. I told him that knowledge was quickly acquired when one understood the purpose of a speech – which, in this case, was making money. On the basis of this essential principle, the statements presented by the various members of the Board on the freezing of soil around a drilling site became easy to understand.

3. ANALYSIS

Interpreting means visualizing the image that has been created, taking a stand, stating emphatically that "that" is what is meant, and even swaying an audience when necessary. In these three respects the interpreter works like a musician or an actor whose art does not merely involve reproduction or repetition, but successful interpretation. The interpreter enjoys greater freedom than the musician or actor since he is not called upon to strike the note indicated by the composer, or to deliver the line written by the playwright. However, he is subject to a greater constraint, since in order to say "the same thing" as the speaker has said in another language, he must comprehend the total message.

Let us leave aside, for the moment, questions involving the role that analysis, memory, comprehension, rapid learning and intelligence play in exploring meaning, and examine the circumstances under which the interpreter works. He is in the situation of both the speaker and the listener and hears the speeches in context. The messages that are exchanged have a purpose which he discerns, and although the medium is oral, and the words vanish as quickly as facial expressions, the meaning lingers on.

Simultaneous and Consecutive Interpretation

In consecutive interpretation the interpreter has the advantage of knowing the line of argument before he interprets. Speeches given at international conferences (excluding written statements)[5] generally last a few minutes, giving the interpreter time to analyze them. He analyzes the nuances and subtleties of the speech, although the message is delivered at a speed averaging 150 words a minute. Few activities require such concentration or cause such fatigue!

Before conference interpreting became commonplace, the speakers offered to stop after every sentence and give the floor to the interpreter. This was a manifestation of the belief that interpre-

---

[5]See Chapter V.5.

tation consisted of a mere word-for-word translation and the speakers felt that, by using this method, the interpreter could commit to memory all of the words in the preceding sentence and then translate them. However, the meaning of an individual sentence is rarely clear when it is taken out of context, and today interpreters request that speakers carry on with their discourse because the rest of the speech will often clarify a statement that was obscure and reveal the assumptions underlying any one sentence.

The time lag that the interpreter enjoys in consecutive interpretation is cruelly lacking in simultaneous interpretation. It may therefore seem inconsistent to claim that simultaneous likewise provides an opportunity for exploration and comprehension of the message. But let us look more closely at simultaneous interpretation before examining the methods of analysis used in interpretation in general.

The observer is struck by the fact that the interpreter manages to do two things at once: listen and speak. But that is not exactly the case. In order to understand what simultaneous interpretation involves, let us look more closely at what happens. When we speak spontaneously our words do not come out in spurts; we do not first think out what we are going to say and then stop thinking while we speak, nor do we stop speaking in order to mentally compose what we are going to say next. On the contrary, our speech is continuous. To be specific, it involves *two superimposed processes* in a cause and effect relationship, mental impulses and their oral expression. Seen in time, however, the words are uttered at the precise moment the following thought is conceived; at the precise moment the product of the conceptualizing process is uttered, the mind is already focused on further development of the thought that is to be expressed in the following statement.

The simultaneous interpreter does virtually the same thing as when he is speaking spontaneously. He hears the next sentence while he is stating the preceding idea, yet he does not *listen* to the next sentence but to the sentence that he himself is delivering. He does, however, *hear the meaning* of the sentence being delivered by the speaker and it is this meaning that he retains in order to deliver the sentence himself immediately afterwards. Thus, just as when he speaks spontaneously, the words he hears while interpreting are those that he utters, but the thoughts that his mind focuses on are those that will produce his next words. The *difference is that, here, the thought he will utter comes from an outside source.*

This is just a very common occurrence carried to extremes. We might go as far as to say that there are no thoughts that are completely the product of one individual, or completely original, and that in any situation what one says is only the end product of a thought that is born of the input of countless outside sources which nourish us as children and enrich us as adults. In practice, however, the simultaneous interpreter is relieved of the immediate task of developing the thought he has just stated. In place of this he substitutes analysis and comprehension of the speaker's line of thought. Simultaneous interpretation involves "hearing" the thoughts of another instead of one's own thoughts. It also involves speaking spontaneously because all speaking involves talking and listening at the same time, although usually one "hears" one's own thoughts. Simultaneous interpretation means reordering the steps in the mental process which we all experience when we speak spontaneously.

This is why, if correctly taught, simultaneous interpretation can be learned quite rapidly, assuming one has already learned the art of analysis in consecutive interpretation. The problem in simultaneous interpretation stems not from the technique used, but from a series of other problems which we shall study in Chapter V under the heading "Interpreting in Practice." Let us simply say here that simultaneous is too often considered as a simple word-for-word translation, with a certain number of words stored in the memory (probably to avoid the trap of false cognates and not translate *actuel* by "actual") and then repeated in the target language. During the time lag that separates the speaker's words from those of the interpreter, the interpreter has better things to do than memorize the words he has heard, because the speaker relentlessly continues to develop his idea and the interpreter must do the same to avoid sputtering out snatches of ideas. Even memorizing a half dozen words would distract the interpreter, whose attention is already divided between listening to his own words and those of the speaker. It would be impossible for him to memorize a certain number of words while uttering the preceding ones in another language. It is humanly impossible to listen attentively to one thing while saying another. The interpreter listens and says the same thing. By avoiding the pitfall of word memorization the interpreter manages to understand the thought that will produce his next words. Thus the simultaneous interpreter is an analyst or mind-reader, not a parrot. His memory *does not store the words* of the sentence delivered by the speaker, but *only the meaning* that those words convey.

Memory

Perhaps the reader will be surprised to see the subject of memory discussed in a chapter entitled "Understanding." It is because, in interpretation, memory and understanding are inseparable; the one is a function of the other.

"Consecutive interpretation must require extraordinary memory," "a photographic memory," participants at international conferences have often told me after having listened to a ten-minute consecutive interpretation. They had the impression that the original speech was preserved, literally, in the interpreter's memory. Although some interpreters do have excellent memories (one of the founders and former presidents of the International Association of Conference Interpreters, A. Kaminker, was reputed to have memorized both parts of Goethe's *Faust*), this impression is misleading because many are not so blessed. They forget telephone numbers, they cannot remember names, they are not at all observant and are incapable of learning anything by heart. And yet all of them, those with good memories and those with bad, render speeches in consecutive interpretation which may last anywhere from three to fifteen minutes (the time necessary to produce from 500 to 2,500 words, or even more) and this is done without summarizing, condensing or paraphrasing, without saying "just anything," and without being inaccurate.

What is useful in interpretation is not the ability to learn something by heart or to remember sounds, figures, words or texts in prose or verse. Studies of memory retention have determined the amount of time necessary for learning to take place, the length of time a memory is retained and the accuracy of recall in relation to the information given. These studies have shown that the less "meaningful" the information, the longer it takes for it to be committed to memory and the harder it is to remember. However, they also reveal that memory is improved if one attaches an imaginary meaning to syllables or figures that lack immediate meaning.

This relationship between meaning and memory can help us to understand how an interpreter remembers. Let us compare the type of memory that allows one to memorize a 500-word passage with the type of memory that would allow a person to remember a full-length film. A person who could almost effortlessly remember what happened in a film would need about an hour to memorize a 500-word passage. (Perhaps he would be unable to recount all the details of the film, but he would know how to reply to any question asking for clarification of details and, for at least a few hours, he could recall the entire film.) Thus there are two types of memory: substantive memory and verbatim memory.

As soon as information is assimilated, it becomes part of substantive memory, whereas it takes about twenty times as long and much repetition to memorize words verbatim (it will take several hours to memorize from 1,500 to 2,000 words, which is the equivalent of 10 to 15 minutes of speaking time).

Substantive memory is the result of rapid analysis which is necessary for complete understanding of the message. In fact, the reason the movie-goer remembers the film is because he understood it. Even though he is not under the same pressure as an interpreter, he too concentrates because he uses two out of his five senses. The information he receives is both visual and auditory and this quite naturally makes him attentive. Furthermore, he is conversant with the various themes found in films, through personal experience, through books or through other media. These themes include love, sickness, travel, jealousy, horses, sheriffs, pretty girls, good and evil. Since all the themes of film are familiar to him, and only their treatment is more or less novel, the movie-goer can easily and fully process the "information" conveyed, and for this reason he remembers, at least for a little while.

It seems clear that substantive memory is a function of comprehension. If, for example, you hear a speech given in a language you do not understand, you can no more remember the speech than you can understand it. Thus, absence of comprehension results in immediate oblivion, whereas comprehension is synonymous with retention. The memory that the interpreter retains of what he has comprehended is of paramount importance both for consecutive interpretation, where he must reproduce information at the end of relatively long speeches, and for simultaneous interpretation, where he lags a bit behind the speaker. In both of these situations he is like the pianist whose hands play the notes of one bar while his eyes are already reading the notes of the next one.

To resist the temptation to rely on verbatim memory, which would be more of a hindrance than a help, the interpreter immediately separates meaning from wording. This separation is extremely important for him since his task is to restate in the target language what has been said in the source language, and thus express it in a structure that is completely different from the original one. It is to his advantage to immediately forget the original wording used since that is not what he will reconstruct, and to clearly retain only the full meaning of the message with all its nuances, just as he remembers not the *tone* of the speaker's delivery, but rather the *meaning* that the tone conveyed.

The interpreter "forgets" the original wording of the message and refuses to mindlessly store a string of hundreds of words in his memory, because he does not "process" wording in the same way as he handles semantic content. You remember something only if you have paid attention to it, if you relate the significance and meaning to your own experience, in short, if you reflect on it in such a way that you experience what is commonly known as "awareness." Memory is much more dependent on what you do with the information than on how your senses perceive it.

While the speaker is speaking, the interpreter concentrates on both his meaning and his wording. When he grasps the meaning, it becomes a part of his active memory; the wording leaves only a faint impression in his memory, lasting just long enough to enable the interpreter to recognize certain words or expressions that may come up again in another speaker's reply.

Thus, the speaker and the interpreter both retain the same information. This fact becomes apparent whenever the speaker understands the language into which his speech is rendered. He is the best judge of the accuracy and completeness of the interpretation, for his judgment is based not on his recollection of what he said, since he has forgotten the exact words he uttered, but on his memory of the meaning of those words. And when he hears his train of thought reproduced he recognizes it. He is then seen to nod his

33

head in approval, smile at his own subtleties, and laugh upon hearing his own jokes come out of the interpreter's mouth.

We can thus see that memory in consecutive interpretation consists of nothing more than understanding the meaning that the words convey. If this understanding is complete and correct, the interpreter will have the transient memory required for the re-expression of information without having to resort to mental gymnastics in order to memorize it.

Moreover, there is a relationship between the speed with which information is assimilated and the length of time it is retained. Information that has been assimilated in the fraction of a second it takes for it to be perceived can only produce a memory of short duration. If it is to become a permanent part of the memory, it will have to be repeated and used a number of times. Herein lies the difference between what is understood and what is absorbed; one is evanescent knowledge and the other is more permanent.

The memory that the movie-goer retains of the movie is short-lived, unless he thinks about it frequently and speaks about it at regular and frequent intervals. In interpretation, memory also lasts only a short time; once the conference is over the interpreter moves on to another one, often changing contexts, subject matters, speakers, etc. This does not mean that he retains absolutely nothing of the knowledge that he acquired temporarily. The interpreter does not erase the memory of a speech from his mind as one erases a recording from a tape in order to record something else. But what was once a part of his active memory seeps into his passive memory. The interpreter is able to confirm or deny the accuracy of information heard at a conference for a much longer time than he can repeat it. Thus, for similar assimilation times, the information contained in the passive memory is retained much longer than that which is contained in the active memory. Information which is vivid in one's mind at the moment when it is perceived is gradually shifted into one's passive memory and can no longer be tapped at will. We are all familiar with the situation where we find ourselves unable to recall somebody's name but nevertheless know immediately whether the name someone else suggests is the name we are looking for or not.

Substantive memory acts the same way in interpretation, i.e., it is either active or passive, and *reactivation of passive memory is one of the essential techniques of interpretation.* Let us consider consecutive interpretation. The image that the description evoked, the meaning brought out by the speaker's position and his style might all be forgotten a few minutes later when his speech is to be interpreted if there is no outside stimulus to reactivate what has become passive knowledge. This is why note-taking is so important in consecutive. You jot down certain key points which indicate the essence of what you will say, just as you tie a knot in your handkerchief to remind you to do something. Consecutive interpretation is a constant exercise in shifting information from passive memory to active memory, both of very short duration. You may actually have understood an idea quite well and have acquired a temporary knowledge of it, but you will still be likely to omit it entirely in your interpretation if it does not appear naturally through association of ideas at the time when it is to be redelivered in consecutive. Yet this idea could be rendered without difficulty if you use a "reminder"; this is what note-taking is used for.

In consecutive interpretation you do not jot down all the details of the unprocessed information (shorthand is never used), but instead you note the results of your meaning analysis. In other words, the interpreter writes down what he intends to say and not what he has heard, just as a panel member jots down a word which will help him to remember the argument he will present in his reply. Note-taking acts as a mnemonic device, a memory aid which triggers the memory of what was understood when heard.

Reactivation of passive memory also serves another function. As he works in very diverse areas, the interpreter acquires extremely varied knowledge. He is not, however, always capable of tapping it at will and it is often necessary for him to reactivate some of it during meetings to make use of it again. To understand how he manages to do this, one must understand the circumstances under which he works. Speakers appear in succession and the interpreter gives them his undivided attention, temporarily converting his permanent passive memory into short-lived active memory. Thus, if it has been several months since he worked at a meeting dealing with magnetic plates, he has the impression that he no longer knows anything about the subject until the moment that the speakers take the floor. At that point he remembers what he understood before and this reactivates his knowledge which, in turn, facilitates his comprehension of the new speech.

In interpretation it is not only knowledge of different *topics* that undergoes this reactivation process. Over the years, interpreters acquire an enormous technical vocabulary but they can only retain a small portion of those *words* in their active memory. The rest are pushed back into passive memory and are not always there when one needs them. (That is why interpreters set up vocabulary card files.) I do not know how many times, when interpreting into French at conferences on metallurgy, I have had to resort to circumlocution to explain the English word "scales" or the German word *Seigerung* because my memory was unable to provide me with the French equivalents, *calamines* and *ségrégation*. However, since the knowledge that is stored in the passive memory is much more permanent than that of active memory, as soon as I heard these two terms mentioned in a speech given in French I knew immediately that these words were the equivalents of "scales" and *Seigerung*. Memory reactivation is, then, quite simple; the interpreter merely has to hear a term a second time and he will remember it until the end of the meeting.

There are certain features of consecutive interpretation, such as proper names, headings and certain numbers, for which message analysis is of no help. If you tried to retain them it would be an exercise in verbatim memory which would hinder the essential analytical task. Thus these words are retained not mentally but on paper. They constitute an important part of the interpreter's notes.

While it is true that the circumstances under which an interpreter works are conducive to comprehension of the message, and that there is nothing unique about the memory he relies on, comprehension is not totally automatic with the interpreter. It is also a deliberate act which is based on a technique.

Spontaneous Comprehension

In order to determine the nature of this technique, let us look once again at our example of the radio broadcast of a sports event. The commentator sees what is happening on the field, understands it and expresses it. His visual perception of the information is reduced to

36

meaning which is, in turn, expressed orally. The conversion of visual information into meaning is a very common process, and also a very unconscious one. We say that we "see Paul," when what we really see is form, color and movement. Only painters pause to examine this visual image. Others understand what they have seen before they have finished looking at it. They relate what they have perceived visually to their previous knowledge about Paul and they have the impression that they have "seen Paul." This process takes place almost unconsciously. A similar process converts auditory perception into meaning. Interpretation is constant proof that comprehension is nothing more than a conversion of information into meaning, which can then be expressed in any given code of communication. If you hear a noise in the sky, you realize that it is made by an airplane passing overhead. The way in which this idea is expressed will depend on the language spoken by the parties involved and on the relationship between the perceived information and the speaker's immediate situation. In this connection, the reader would probably accept the idea that *there are as many ways to express a concept as there are languages on earth and contexts for the message*. Reasoning along these same lines, we could further accept the idea that, regardless of the language in which it is expressed, any oral communication can be reduced to the meaning of the message it conveys. Thus interpretation is a triangular process and not simply a linear process of transfer from one language to another. The language is perceived (perception stage), reduced to meaning (comprehension stage), and finally expressed in another linguistic form (expression stage).

To put it metaphorically, we could say that, if the interpreter works from French into English, he reduces the French cloth to shreds, cards the material and reweaves it into English cloth. In other words, before restating what he hears, the interpreter reduces the speaker's formulated thought to an unformulated thought. Once this is done there is nothing to prevent him from expressing the thought, which is now his own, just as spontaneously as he expresses his own ideas when he is not interpreting.

In this way the interpreting process is not inherently different from the process that every human being goes through every day whenever he formulates his thoughts. The mental process used by an interpreter grows out of constant, daily practice. He uses the faculty that every human being possesses to understand an infinite number of ideas and to store them non-verbally (which has nothing to do with memorizing words or learning something by heart); he can then express thoughts and concepts in a verbal form, which appears spontaneously when voiced and vanishes just as quickly. Much of the interpreter's technique is thus based on a spontaneous mental process — the thought-language process. Looking more closely at this, we can see that the process is reversible and that, when reversed, this process produces comprehension. What does this mean? It means that the words "I see Paul" heard by an outsider are *understood* because that outsider reduces the name of Paul to a vague mental image, and that he moves from the oral expression to thought in order to understand what he was told.

If we carry this study of the relationship between thought and language a bit further, we find another similarity with the field of interpretation. We have discussed the thought-language process as well as the reverse language-thought process, yet neither thought nor language is static. We have seen how one word can conjure up a vast range of meanings, and also how thought, at the other end of the process, finds countless ways in which to express itself. If we examine this dynamic relationship more closely, we realize that there is a constant interaction between language and thought. Anyone who expresses himself finds that the words he utters inspire thought, clarify it and develop it. Language, therefore, *simultaneously expresses and generates thought.* There is a constant two-way flow between the thought impulses, which inspire the words, and the words, which inspire new thoughts. The consequent discourse is the result of the exchanges between shapeless thought and speech. Compared to this thought-language-thought process, the uniqueness of interpretation lies only in the fact that, before formulating "his" thought, the interpreter appropriates the thought of another person. We might say that interpreting is a process of speech-thought-speech, in which the words of the speaker become the thought of the interpreter and are then reconverted into speech by him.

An interpreter's understanding can work in two ways, through spontaneous processes or through deliberate acts. The former, which we have just analyzed, are basically a function of the interpreter's intelligence and the degree of his awareness of the technique (because the interpreter who attempts to translate word for word hinders and inhibits the spontaneity of his understanding). To a lesser degree, they are also a function of the similarity of the interpreter's and the speaker's mental structures. The interpreter understands much better when he has an affinity with the speaker's mental functioning. The line of reasoning that he hears then seems logical to him.

No matter how intelligible a message may be, it can be completely understood only with the help of the person to whom it is addressed. In order for this to happen, the listener must be willing to receive the message, consider it and meet the speaker at least part way.

However, only certain parts of the message that is delivered to the passive listener (the type of listener present at public meetings) get through. Some parts of the message do not interest him and therefore are ignored. Other parts reach him and hold his attention for a certain amount of time, and therefore other information goes unnoticed. As for the active listener (the participant at a conference), he listens to what is said while mentally preparing the arguments he will use to confirm or rebut what he has heard. The arguments heard serve as a pretext for the development of individual arguments and thus his attention is also divided, since it is focused on both what he hears and what he is going to say. He ignores certain trivial or odd-sounding statements and retains those to which he has reacted. This reaction directs his attention to certain ideas, which he focuses on, analyzes and replies to, while ignoring others; he spontaneously concentrates on certain points. The listener remembers what has impressed him and this serves as a point of departure for his argument. He retains only the ideas that have served as a springboard for his own thoughts. What he remembers of what the other person said actually depends on his own reaction.

This relationship between the speaker and the listener is derived from the process we have already described whereby language generates thought. This relationship is just as operative when the thoughts are one's own as when they come from an outside source. This process corresponds to *spontaneous comprehension* and it allows a dialogue to take place even if part of the message goes unnoticed.

Concentration: A Conscious Act

The effort of concentration required of the interpreter is completely different. What is normal in a dialogue situation no longer applies when it comes to interpreting because the interpreter, interposed between the speaker and the listener, must comprehend *all of the speech* in order to transmit it without omitting, distorting or adding anything. It is only by transmitting *everything* to the listener that the interpreter gives him the opportunity to sort out what interests him and use it to sustain a dialogue.

In order to understand everything, the interpreter relies on more than just the process of spontaneous comprehension. He must consciously analyze all of the message, in a way that is more intuitive than verbal and, of course, he must do this quickly. There must be a deliberate division of thought; he allows enough associations of ideas to emerge in his own mind to enable him to grasp the message, but he does not develop them into his own ideas. He focuses his attention on all the nuances contained in the statement and at the same time holds back the development of the thoughts that they inspire. If he did not make this conscious effort to listen to everything that was said, but instead listened only to what interested him, it is clear that he would not "hear" even half of what was said. This capacity for concentrated listening, accompanied by immediate analysis which reduces language to the meaning of its message, is one of the most important requirements for conference interpreting and one of the rarest qualities around. It keeps the interpreter from reacting like the listeners who ignore certain parts of the message. If the interpreter relied purely on spontaneous comprehension he would transmit a partial message, stressing points that *he* thought were important.

If, however, he completely refused to associate ideas, and ceased to analyze, he would replace interpretation with a rough, literal translation, and would convey an unrefined message that would force the listener to attempt to reconstruct the meaning and prevent him from reflecting on the message and reacting to what was said.

Thus the interpreter does not receive a message passively. He actively analyzes each and every part of it and only with regard to minor points does he take the liberty of keeping what is worthwhile and dropping what is not (repetitions, slips of the tongue, etc.).

The density of the message that the interpreter assimilates is much greater than the listener realizes. This total assimilation of the message requires a degree of *concentration* rarely seen, a deliberate selection and elimination of sensory perceptions, with their corresponding mental images. Among the half dozen perceptions and ideas that our mind has to grapple with simultaneously in all kinds of situations in everyday life, we manage to sift through, select and give priority to those items of information that we consider most important, ignoring the rest. People scarcely notice a radio playing when they are discussing something, whereas the ringing of the telephone interrupts a conversation; we are accustomed to blocking out certain types of noises in order to concentrate on things that are of immediate concern. When he interprets, the interpreter is under pressure. He therefore gives priority to outside information over his own thoughts and other possible distractions.

It should be pointed out that even the best interpreters would be incapable of doing "cold" what they manage to do at a meeting. The interpreter is there with his listeners; he sees them and his words are intended for their ears. Furthermore, in consecutive interpretation, he has to give his speech immediately after the speaker finishes his; in simultaneous he must switch on his microphone as soon as the speaker begins to talk. This in itself would be a source of stage fright for many, and would leave them speechless; yet for the interpreter it is a stimulus that allows him to carry out the intense work of analysis needed in order to grasp what is implied. This mental exercise is exceptional because it takes place with split-second speed. Thus we can say that interpretation approaches the creative possibilities of original thought.

Moreover, the audience that the interpreter addresses is not *a priori* trusting or charitable, for the interpreter has none of the built-in advantages of those who usually speak in public. He is not a teacher who addresses his students and enjoys the prestige his position affords him, nor is he a lecturer who has the double psychological advantage of addressing an audience that wants to hear what he has to say, and also of knowing more than they do.

The interpreter is well aware that his listeners will note only the problems he may run into with terminology and that, most often, the inner workings of the interpretation process will completely escape them. They will tend to be louder in their praise for the consecutive

41

interpretation of an after-dinner speech than for the simultaneous interpretation of remarks concerning the most complex subjects; the more knowledgeable they are about a given subject, the more critical they will be. This position of relative inferiority increases the stress under which an interpreter works. Knowing that he must win his listeners over, he succeeds in analyzing in a few micro-seconds what would take him very much longer to accomplish outside the context of a meeting.

When learning their profession, interpretation students are faced with countless problems: an idea may stump them because of its novelty, the language may be too obscure, they may be paralyzed with stage fright or they may not concentrate hard enough on what they are hearing. Here are two examples that illustrate this.

In an interpretation exam, the students were required to interpret a speech by Pierre Mendès-France which contained the following passage:

> *Partout où il y a action collective: BATAILLE, construction d'un immeuble, organisation d'une entreprise privée ou publique... il faut un plan pour déterminer les conditions d'exécution les meilleures − sinon c'est le gaspillage et finalement l'échec.*[6]

This text was interpreted six times that morning and not one of the students translated *BATAILLE*. Why was it omitted? The word would have been extremely easy to translate if it had been frozen in a written text, but it was oral, and too unexpected in this context to be understood by inexperienced young people. When questioned afterwards, the students all remember having heard the word but to them *bataille* evoked the idea of conflict rather than solidarity, and they were unable to translate it because they had not understood it. They did not understand it because they failed to make the proper associations. We would add here that we consider this example to

---

[6]"Wherever collective effort is involved − *battles*, construction sites, establishing public enterprises or private corporations − a plan is needed to determine the best way to set about the task at hand. Otherwise, the result is a squandering of resources, and ultimate failure."

42

be striking proof of the existence of the triangular process in interpretation, i.e., speech-meaning-speech, where the meaning and not the words are translated. Because the meaning of the word was not understood, it could not be translated.

The second example involved young Tunisians who were listening to an American agricultural instructor. He was describing the qualities and knowledge necessary to be a good agricultural extension agent. He listed several factors which included, among other things, knowledge of soils, animal pathology and *faith in God*. All of these young people had been educated under the French system and none of them could bring himself to repeat "faith in God," which seemed so out of place in this context. When questioned about this later, they recalled having heard the words "faith in God" but they had not *understood* what was meant.

So the mere fact that information is heard does not guarantee that it will be included in the interpretation. Analysis for interpretation requires interrelating the constituent parts of the speech to the point where the entire speech forms a coherent whole and nothing is omitted.

TECHNIQUES OF ANALYSIS

Reference to Pre-existing Knowledge

We said earlier that, in order to understand for purposes of interpretation, one must reduce language to the meaning it conveys, and that hearing the name "Paul" involves dimly visualizing a conceptual image of Paul. We further stated that interpreting involves comprehension of the entire speech through a process that is half spontaneous and half deliberate. Let us now look at how one moves from language to meaning by referring, once again, to the example of Paul, and analyzing the process that makes us believe that we have seen him. We only see a figure but we *know* that this figure is Paul. In order to say that we have seen Paul we relate the new information to our pre-existing knowledge, the connection is made immediately and comprehension is the equivalent of *renewed knowledge*. If the gap between the new information and our pre-existing knowledge is too large, the connection is never made and understanding does not take place. In other words, if you did not know Paul before you saw him you would not know it was Paul you saw. Comprehension is what occurs when new information ties in with related knowledge. If such knowledge is absent the new information is ignored. The intense analysis that is a part of the interpretation process results from the need to assimilate the complete message, which means linking up new information with relatively unrelated knowledge.

Every item of information brings to mind a vast semantic range, as we saw in the case of our plumber. When the semantic range that the speaker's words awaken in the mind of the listener overlaps with the listener's pre-existing semantic range, *knowledge is reactivated.* If the overlapping is slight and if one must reconstruct the whole of the semantic field from this small fragment, actual invention or discovery can take place. Interpretation does not go quite as far as discovery, but it does proceed in the same direction.

It is not necessary to awaken the entire semantic range but one must open up enough to understand the information received. By applying logical thought processes, it is possible to go beyond immediate superficial comprehension and link up information (which at first seemed incomprehensible) with knowledge that is sometimes more closely related to other areas. One quickly realizes, when teaching interpretation, that a student who says "I don't understand" when he hears a technical passage really means "I don't know what they are talking about." He naturally refuses to make a special effort, which would amount to reducing the technical information to an understandable, popularized version. It would of course be highly personalized, since the individual involved would be its only user, but this approach clearly describes how one can link up the most specialized type of information with the relatively basic knowledge that one has of the subject matter.

Let us take an example involving the Concorde. The man on the street has heard that this supersonic plane can cross the Atlantic in three hours. In order for this information to be meaningful for him he must have some prior knowledge about the length of time it takes other planes to cross the Atlantic, which he can then relate to the new information. He will then see, immediately, that the Concorde will be faster than a Boeing 747. If, however, he has no previous knowledge of the subject he will not be able to come to this conclusion and he will miss the point.

Let us consider another example. Suppose you learn at a conference that the wheat crop in a particular country has been poor, which is something you did not know before the conference. But you did already know that that same country produces significant quantities of gold. You can then understand why the conference predicts that the price of gold on the London market will drop. Using your pre-existing knowledge, you reason (a) that the country is buying cereals for gold and (b) that this is why the price of gold is expected to drop. This comprehension becomes knowledge that will aid the interpreter in understanding additional information.

When we state that analysis for the purpose of understanding involves associating incoming information with pre-existing knowledge, we define knowledge as all things known, even if the knowledge was acquired the instant before. Thus we could say that all information, once understood, becomes acquired knowledge which allows the interpreter to develop his analysis. In fact, although the speaker is not a teacher addressing students and does not move gradually from material that is known to material that is unknown, but is instead a specialist communicating with colleagues, his message always contains information that can be readily acquired as knowledge.

The interpreter immediately understands certain parts of the information, he is obliged to analyze others, and thus, in the course of the meeting, he acquires the requisite temporary knowledge that allows him to gradually close the initial gap between himself and the speaker, thereby facilitating his analysis.

In his analysis, the interpreter does not limit himself to linking the message to his pre-existing knowledge, but *he also analyzes the interrelationships within the message itself.* He knows that he can only understand the message if it appears coherent to him. Here is an anecdote that circulated among interpreters at the time of the disturbances in Congo-Kinshasa. A United Nations plane had been circling for an hour over a landing strip. One of the passengers, who was an interpreter, asked the Belgian liaison officer what was happening and was told, *Le pilote* ne sait pas *atterrir*.[7] The inter-

---

[7]"The pilot does not know how to land."

preter was unfamiliar with this Belgian use of *savoir*[8] where the French would use *pouvoir*[9] and thought that he had just been told that the pilot was incompetent. But his fear was quickly dispelled by his speedy analysis which led him to conclude that, since the pilot knew how to take off, he must know how to land. Since he understood that he had been misled by this unusual use of the word, the interpreter correctly asked, "Isn't the runway clear?"

The deliberate act of comprehension encompasses even the most ordinary information. When someone says that a satellite reaches the highest point in its orbit when it is 750 kilometers away from the earth, the interpreter does not let this number go by without understanding it, i.e., visualizing the distance. By thinking of an analogous distance, for example, the approximate distance between Paris and Toulouse, the interpreter will not make the stupid mistake of saying 75 kilometers or 7,500 kilometers when he transmits the information.

Analysis becomes so much a part of the interpreter's thought process that he uses it all the time, as when he questions the simple logic or likelihood of an item of information that has appeared in the newspaper, or when he cannot rest until he is satisfied that he has understood some aspect of another culture. I remember a meeting in Addis Ababa that took place shortly after the Queen of England's visit to Ethiopia. Outside of the meeting, one of the participants at the conference said that the route to be taken by the Queen had been lined with trees specially for the occasion and added, with a derisive smile, that three days later the trees had withered and that surely the Queen had not been fooled. I was amused by the reply given by one of my colleagues who remarked that the tree planting had undoubtedly been done to pay homage to the Queen as a sort of gigantic bouquet of flowers, and was not intended to deceive her. This explanation seemed logical and it proved to be the right answer. Thus the interpreter always walks the thin line between logic and likelihood.

---

[8]"To know."

[9]To be able to.

The Interpreter's Stance

Message analysis often involves another element of comprehension: the interpreter's own views with respect to the argument presented.

We do not need elaborate arguments to defend the interpreter's right to have views of his own. Since his personal thoughts are not articulated, they can be radically different from the speaker's. The interpreter is often harsh in his judgment, just as harsh as the notes a reader writes in the margin of a book indicating the passages that have pleased or offended him. It is this judgment that molds his understanding and allows him to relate the arguments he hears to his pre-existing knowledge.

In the interests of shedding some light on this process, let us look at the interpreter's attitude by examining a specific example. The following passage is an excerpt from a speech given during a conference on the training of journalists: "We are amazed, as are many others, that recruitment *into a profession which is one of the most complex and one of those which carry the greatest social responsibility*, has been — and continues to be — left to chance and even made according to the wrong criteria."

Here we shall only analyze how the interpreter manages to retain the two characteristics attributed to the profession of journalism which shape the meaning of the entire message: (1) it is one of the most complex and (2) it is one of those that carry the greatest social responsibility. The interpreter might agree with the first statement because he sees a certain similarity between interpretation and journalism. By comparing his job to that of the journalist he has "taken a stand" and this will be sufficient to enable him to remember what was said. Let us suppose, however, that he does not agree with the second statement and that, in his eyes, the journalist is no decision maker and has little responsibility when compared to a politician, for instance, whose very purpose is action. The interpreter feels that the journalist takes advantage of not being in a responsible position to say exactly what he pleases. Even if he does not carry his analysis through, the fact that he notes his own disagreement, takes an opposing viewpoint, and reacts to what was said by taking a stand, ensures that he will accurately reproduce the speaker's thought.

Thus by taking a stand for or against an argument he hears, the interpreter understands the argument more thoroughly, remembers it and can give it back. The interpreter's analysis and the reasons for his agreement or disagreement will not show through in his translation, because the more conscious the interpreter is of what has been said, the more aware he is of the difference between his own point of view and that of the speaker. Sometimes disagreement can take the form of a mental exclamation mark and agreement is registered as amusement; but in interpretation, an interpreter can never remain neutral with respect to an argument, for if he did, he might forget or distort it.

When you observe interpreters at work, you notice that they sometimes feel the need to make observations, to add a footnote to what the speaker says; an interpreter at work will turn to his colleague and whisper a comment which the latter usually fails to understand because he has not been listening attentively to the speaker.

It is when he analyzes abstract reasoning and grasps the line of argument in a message that the interpreter truly merits his name, because he performs an exegesis of it for himself before transmitting it. But among all the exchanges that take place at international conferences the interpreter has to deal with more than just abstract messages. *Descriptive* style abounds, and the effort needed to comprehend description is not the same as that needed to understand concatenations of ideas. Here it is no longer a question of analyzing but of *visualizing*.

Visualization

Let us imagine that we have to interpret the following passage:

> The whine of the engines increased in intensity, signaling the approach of the presidential jet. Then the Caravelle landed, gracefully and lightly. The sun glittered on the wings, making them sparkle. The president emerged, his features drawn with fatigue, and greeted the crowd of onlookers who had come to the airport out of curiosity.

Aside from the arrival of a president, not much else happened. The interpreter hears a description whose elements are known and only has to pay attention to how they are put together. The

description itself can be reduced to images without any difficulty whatsoever.

The mental image that the interpreter visualizes upon hearing the description abounds with details of the airplane, the sun, the airport and the crowd. This in turn allows him to evoke the same image in the target language without remembering the words that described it. His experience with sun and heads of state probably does not exactly fit the event described, but it is sufficient to allow him to express an image that will evoke the same mental picture in the minds of his listeners that they would have gotten from the original commentator.

The image that the interpreter obtains from the words he hears is thus colored by his own experience and is not exactly the same as the experience that inspired the original words. The conceptual image that the interpreter visualizes and converts into language will similarly evoke an image in the minds of those listening to him; the image they visualize will be colored by their own experiences, but the image may well correspond to the image they would have visualized if they had heard the original words.

The interpreter's image may be very different from the speaker's because the interpreter may not possess the speaker's and listener's specialized knowledge of the subject. The interpreter's careful analysis is, however, sufficient to enable him to evoke the original image in the mind of the listener. He is helped in this task by the fact that the listener and the speaker share the same sphere of knowledge. Allow me to explain. If an archaeologist were to say to a colleague (through an interpreter), "I discovered a beautiful bracelet in a Punic tomb," the interpreter who had never seen an excavation would undoubtedly visualize bracelets and tombs that would be very different from the actual Punic ones. Yet the image he would create would evoke the correct image in the mind of the other archaeologist.

Thus, although the image that the interpreter visualizes to aid his own understanding is not necessarily identical with that of the speaker, it allows him to correctly relay the image that the speaker visualized.

Upon hearing the speaker's words, the interpreter is reminded of certain images, functions, and cause and effect relationships, which he associates with the ones he is hearing. This allows him to understand that which is unknown to him and which has been only partially elucidated by the speaker.

However, even when he understands, the interpreter is still only a listener or, at most, a participant for himself alone. He makes no judgments on the soundness of the argument being presented because he does not know all the elements of the situation and only uses the analogy he draws to reconstruct the argument he has heard.

The technique used in interpretation to relay a descriptive message, i.e., visual imagination, is relatively easy to apply provided the described object or a similar one is known to the interpreter. Understanding a descriptive message thus requires *greater knowledge* than is required to understand a line of argument. But the technique is less involved because it does not require quite as thorough an analysis.

There is another type of description which does not lend itself so readily to the creation of mental imagery; it involves a *series of events*, none of which is described in detail. In such cases one tries to understand the successive stages in the development of events. Consequently, if a speaker says that "Family X made a fortune in Algeria, sent its money home when the disorders broke out, started a publishing house in Paris, and began to publish a quarterly magazine in 1962, which became a monthly in January 1964," the image left in one's mind would not be comprehensive but fragmented into a string of rapidly sketched images connected by the cause and effect relationship that binds together the different stages of the description.

A conscious analysis of a descriptive speech involves bringing out its images, and noting the stages of its development. This conscious analysis allows us to take an active interest in what was said and to relate what was said to what we already know in order to understand. In any case, it is imperative that the interpreter maintain an active interest during each stage of the description in order to be able to reproduce it accurately in the target language.

Observing Style

To complete our treatment of the subject, let us take a look at another type of speech: the emotional speech. Its purpose is to elicit laughter, to please, to extend thanks, to praise, etc. These speeches are delivered as after-dinner speeches, opening remarks, funeral orations, all of which the interpreter classifies as "blah-blah-blah." This type of speech is the most difficult to analyze because all one has to work with is the objective of the person speaking. Instead of bringing out the logic of an argument, or attempting to visualize images, the interpreter turns his attention to the motives and the style of the speaker. He makes it a point to remember a particular descriptive expression and to note whether the tone of the speech is friendly or critical and adjusts his tone accordingly. In this type of speech the subtleties of style are very important.

This is the type of speech where the beginning interpreter trusts his memory least and where he takes the most notes. But the seasoned interpreter knows a number of ready-made formulas, for he has heard them so often in so many contexts that they come to mind automatically.

We should remember that the distinction made between different types of speeches is never as sharp in practice as this discussion might suggest. It would be difficult to imagine an after-dinner speech that would not require the interpreter to visualize images or take a stand on an argument, in addition to having to analyze the speaker's motivations and observe his style. Conversely, it would be difficult to imagine a declaratory speech that did not make some type of emotional appeal, or a descriptive speech that contained no progression of ideas.

In fact, although we have, for the purposes of analysis, isolated the elements which are found to varying degrees in all speeches, they are intimately related and sometimes appear together in the same sentence. Thus — for the interpreter — analysis, images, attitude, highlighting of stylistic nuances intertwine and overlap in a speech, even if the general tone of the speech shows a decided preference for one type of message.

***

Thus we have begun to see how different the process of interpretation is from the commonly held ideas that we mentioned at the beginning of this book. Far from being a rote translation of the words of a speech, interpretation involves the immediate forgetting of words. By ignoring the wording of the message, the interpreter can turn all his attention to analyzing the content of what he has heard in order to understand it in its entirety. His analysis can be viewed as a reaction to the message or, if you prefer, the taking of a stand. Comprehension, far from being a secondary tool of the interpreter, a type of intellectual luxury which he may occasionally allow himself, is in reality the very basis of his work. One could say *interpreting is first and foremost comprehension.*

The term comprehension, however, is ambiguous because it covers many areas. One could "comprehend" all the words in a message without comprehending its meaning and, conversely, understand a message without having understood all of the words. We hope we have shown how the interpreter understands and how his understanding differs from that of the speaker and listener. We must now examine the two principal elements that are indispensable for immediate and comprehensive understanding. To understand what is going on around him, every individual depends on two types of knowledge in his daily life: *knowledge of words and knowledge of things.* Given the special circumstances under which he works, the interpreter finds these two types of knowledge of primary importance. We will examine them in more detail in the following chapters and determine the kind of understanding needed for interpretation.

CHAPTER III

KNOWLEDGE

1. THE SUBJECT MATTER

In order to stand a good chance of understanding what is being said, the interpreter must have some knowledge of the subject under discussion. In attempting to highlight the basic processes involved in interpretation, we have perhaps left the reader with the impression that knowledge is not necessary in order to interpret. This is just as untrue as thinking that interpreters are specialists in the subjects that they deal with at the conferences where they work.[1] The interpreter must have sufficient knowledge of the field being discussed to be able to analyze it intelligently, but it is not necessary for him to have an expert's knowledge of the subject. Comprehension and knowledge are two different things.

Specialists and Generalists

Outside the field of interpretation, these two concepts, knowledge and comprehension, are rarely differentiated. One seeks to understand what one does not know, in order to assimilate it and, conversely, one only understands immediately what one already knows. This is clearly evident during one's schooling and university studies and later in one's professional life, which is generally geared to one specific area. It is also evident in private life, where one rarely ventures into areas that are totally alien. For the expert, the line between knowledge and understanding often becomes quite blurred because the rather circumscribed knowledge gained early in life simply becomes deeper, not wider.

The interpreter is not in the same category as the specialist. In his profession he is not the *initiator of information*, as is the foreman

---

[1]See Annex I for a sample list of the wide variety of conference topics.

giving instructions or the teacher standing in front of the class. He is *presented with information*. He is not the one who advances an opinion, introduces new information or reacts to a statement. All he does is receive this information. No matter how knowledgeable he may be on the subject, it would be unthinkable for him to replace something the speaker said with his own ideas or thoughts on the subject. To accurately render what the speaker says, he must wait until he has heard it; thus even if the interpreter working at a medical conference is himself a physician, he will not know exactly *what* the speaker will say before he says it. Thus this kind of knowledge (i.e., that needed by the specialist *originating* the information) is something he will never possess. What is, however, indispensable for the interpreter is to understand the information. As he gains experience in his profession, he becomes an expert at analysis and exegesis, rather than becoming an expert in any one specific field.

The interpreter is a generalist in the same way that judges in arbitration courts and politicians are generalists. The former are trained in law, yet they settle cases that involve a wide range of technologies; the latter deal with numerous facets of life in their countries. Both use their intelligence not to originate information, but to organize it in a rational manner.

The generalist must understand everything, but to do so he need not possess the knowledge of a specialist. One can understand the need for anastomosis (uniting of vessels or hollow organs) in surgery without knowing how to perform the operation or even how to describe it; yet a rudimentary knowledge of anatomy is necessary in order to understand what is said. To understand that a reactor goes critical once its reactivity coefficient exceeds 1.0 requires some basic scientific instruction, but one does not have to be a nuclear physicist. One can easily follow an argument recommending mineral additives in cattle feed, or accept the idea that nitrogen and potassium chloride improve soil fertility, and understand a subsequent line of reasoning based on this fact, without being an agronomist or a chemist.

The specialist draws from his knowledge when discussing the advantages and disadvantages of a particular technical process. In a meeting, he listens to a speaker's rationale and prepares a response based on his knowledge of the subject matter. The interpreter, in his ignorance, does not judge the soundness of the arguments being presented nor does he judge the accuracy, the originality or the cogency of the message, but he does understand what the message seeks to prove. To do so, his level of *knowledge* need not be identical to that of the speaker, but he must have a *comparable level of intellectual ability*. He is faithful to the speaker chiefly through logical analysis and only secondarily through his knowledge of the subject. It is his power of reasoning, rather than his command of the facts, that must be on a par with that of the speaker.

Intellectual Level

Participants at international conferences are men and women of achievement, of importance in their field. One must have acquired a certain reputation to be designated to defend the position of one's government or corporation, labor union or institute at an international conference, or to present research findings.

The same selection criteria hold for interpreters, because understanding a message means understanding the train of thought of the conference delegate and therefore having an intellectual ability comparable to his and a mind that is just as keen. So although their sphere of knowledge may be quite disparate, generalists and specialists share a similar intellectual endowment and meet on an intellectual level. It is just as important to distinguish between the type of knowledge of a generalist and that of a specialist.

It is, of course, inconceivable that you could understand something about which you are totally ignorant, since understanding, as we have seen, is the merging of new pieces of information with previously acquired knowledge or experience. Consequently, however intense the reasoning effort, it is impossible to make the necessary association of ideas if there is no prior knowledge on which to build. In order to analyze what is said and to understand it, the interpreter must raise his level of understanding of the subject to a level which, while far from equaling that of the specialist, will be distinctly higher than that of the ordinary educated person. The acquisition of this knowledge takes place both *before* and *during* the conference.

Acquisition of Knowledge

In preparing for a conference of dermatology, for example, the interpreter must first digest the fundamentals to be found in a ready-reference series or introductory handbook on — in this case — the skin. To understand why liquid sodium is used as a coolant in nuclear reactors and what problems this gives rise to, one must know what a heat exchanger is, but one must also study up on problems of corrosion.

This information can be assimilated very rapidly. The interpreter does not prepare for a conference in the same way as he prepared for an exam in his student days, since he does not have to use this knowledge actively. However, it should be readily available and spring to mind spontaneously once the discussion gets under way.

You may well wonder whether this knowledge will enable the interpreter to work in an infinite variety of fields. After all, depending on the country in which they are trained, lawyers are required to study for 3 or 4 years, physicians for 6 or 7 years and engineers for 4 or 5 years. Moreover, once they have earned their professional degrees, their knowledge is still not complete, since before they are able to perform their job properly they must bridge the gap between academic knowledge and practical experience by on-the-job training. It is also true that practicing engineers, physicians, etc. are often overwhelmed by the rapid expansion of knowledge in their fields and feel the need for academic refresher courses.

If we assume that the interpreter is intelligent and has mastered the techniques of interpretation, the knowledge he possesses will serve as a foundation for his understanding because this knowledge was acquired in a rational, logical manner, which will stand him in infinitely better stead than rote learning or imitation. It is this analytical habit of mind that allows him to rapidly acquire additional knowledge on the topic to be discussed and to assimilate basic concepts in highly specialized fields in a matter of hours.

Let us not forget that conferences are encounters between specialists who share a pool of common knowledge and who meet to discuss only limited aspects of their already narrow field. A medical conference does not deal with medicine in general but thoroughly probes specific topics, for example, "Early Screening of Silicosis," or "Skin Grafts of Small Lesions." Although in theory interpretation covers a wide range of fields, in practice only a minute portion of the sum total of human knowledge is actually discussed at any given conference.

We could compare the infinite variety of knowledge to which an interpreter might be exposed with the limitless possible combinations of shapes and colors in a kaleidoscope, in which any individual meeting corresponds to a temporary freezing of the movement of the kaleidoscope where the images and colors are all brought into sharp focus.

Knowledge is also acquired *during the course of a meeting*. Every time the interpreter works at a conference, every time he tackles a subject, he learns something new. The more experienced he is in the mental exercise of analysis, the more quickly he assimilates the kind of information that will facilitate his task. Each statement made at a conference is a source of knowledge and information. Whenever the merging of new information with prior knowledge lights the spark of understanding, whether in conjunction with material acquired for the conference or by matching up with information in a completely different sphere, the interpreter stretches his mind and enhances his knowledge.

To illustrate how much can be learned at a conference, take the example of a meeting of stockholders in a potash mining company. What the interpreter knows prior to the meeting is that potash is used to make fertilizer. At the conference he learns that there are potash mines in Zaire, Alsace in France, and Saskatchewan in Canada. By putting together various bits and pieces of information gleaned in the course of the meeting, he deduces that, in order to sink shafts, the ground must be frozen, and that cement is grouted in to strengthen the walls. As the meeting progresses the subject becomes increasingly familiar to him and the likelihood that he will misunderstand certain items of information decreases.

Knowledge acquired during meetings is not as coherent as that which is acquired by the interpreter before the meeting. After a few years of interpreting experience, the snatches of disparate information nevertheless add up to a sum total of knowledge that is stored almost unconsciously, but which the interpreter taps constantly whenever he approaches new subjects.

Too Much or Too Little Knowledge

There are cases where neither advance preparation nor knowledge acquired during the conference is sufficient to bridge the gap between the experts' knowledge and the amount of knowledge that the interpreter needs to understand what is being said. In such cases, it is impossible to interpret in the way we have defined it, i.e., to give a full and accurate rendering of the meaning of the speech. There is no denying that such situations do occur and interpreting then becomes what it is generally believed to be: mere rote reproduction of words in another language. That kind of interpretation is of dubious assistance to conference delegates. I remember a meeting of chemists where the corrosion of nuclear containers was being discussed. Insufficient knowledge of chemistry prevented me from grasping the rationale behind the speakers' words, and I had to fall back on a sentence-by-sentence translation, repeating chemical formulae that were meaningless to me.

Thus, whenever the gap between the interpreter's knowledge of the subject and that of the expert is too great or has not been sufficiently reduced by knowledge acquired before or during the conference, comprehension is sketchy at best.

Chemistry and mathematics are probably the subjects that lend themselves least to real interpretation, because to a large extent they use jargon that is different from ordinary speech and from which it is impossible to derive any meaning if one's command of the jargon is not as good as one's mastery of the source and target languages. To a lesser extent, this is also true for medicine, for those interpreters who have never studied Greek or Latin. These are fields where literal translation is possible, where a word has an exact equivalent in the other language, and where problems of interpretation are due as much — if not more — to unfamiliarity with the specialized language used as to a lack of subject knowledge.

Thus, assuming equal difficulty of subject matter, a medical paper presented in German is much more *understandable* than one in French or English, because it uses only one language, German, and the constituent parts of the word help explain its meaning. When you hear the words *rechtsdrehender* or *linksdrehender Stärke-zucker*, you understand more than when you hear "dextrose" or "levulose." Similarly, *Stoffwechsel* is more descriptive than "metabolism," and the same is true for "river-blindness" as compared to the word "onchocerciasis" used by specialists.

On the other hand, it is obviously easier to reproduce scientific words with Greek or Latin roots in English or other languages that commonly use Greek- or Latin-based scientific terminology (*métabolisme* - "metabolism"; *dextrose* - "dextrose"). Thus the closer the vocabulary of the two languages, the more literal the interpretation and the less analytical the interpreter can be. At a conference on pharmacology, for example, the French-English interpreters can practically forgo all preparation of the subject matter, while those working into German must possess considerable knowledge of the field.

Occasionally a specialist in a given subject who also happens to be "multilingual" will volunteer or be co-opted to interpret for a meeting in his field. This is a case where the specialized knowledge of the person doing the interpreting is at least on a par with that of the other participants. And yet these ad-hoc interpreters fail where the professional interpreter succeeds, because they run into a different problem. Their concentration tends to slacken, and hence there is a falling off of the intense analysis which is indispensable to an understanding of the specific message the speaker seeks to convey: the amateur interpreter's knowledge of the field can actually prove a handicap to understanding, if it causes him to jump to his own conclusions rather than analyzing the speaker's words and if the mental matching up of prior knowledge and new information is only cursory. Let us recall that when we speak of the interpreter's knowledge we mean a body of information that to a greater or lesser extent coincides with that of the speaker, but is never knowledge of precisely *what* the speaker is going to say. Yet it is his specific message that must be understood, and for this purpose an expert in analysis may prove more effective than a subject specialist.

It is curious to note how prior knowledge can hinder the acquisition of new knowledge. We display a certain mental laziness when exposed to unfamiliar information, tending to equate it automatically with prior knowledge, and we are thus blinded to genuinely new information. By way of illustration we would point to the difficulty that a person experiences, after a certain age, in pronouncing the sounds of a foreign language. He focuses too heavily on the way the letters are sounded in his own language, instead of trying to sound out the words according to their own phonetic pattern.

The Interpreter's Knowledge: A Means to an End

Perhaps one of the keys to why interpretation succeeds is to be found in the circumstances under which the interpreter must work. He is constantly forced to understand problems about which he knows little and this stimulates his curiosity and furthers an open-minded attitude; he knows he is ignorant of many things; he sees knowledge as a dynamic process; he continually challenges what he hears and is satisfied only by information that makes sense.

But the line between comprehension and knowledge becomes blurred for someone who is knowledgeable about a subject, and the interpreter's ability to be a *mediator of meaning* is generally viewed with some skepticism by those whose speeches he interprets. It is precisely because participants at international conferences are so thoroughly convinced that interpretation is a simple word-for-word translation that they are at a loss to provide the interpreter with the explanation he sometimes requests.

An LNG (liquefied natural gas) tanker uses "boil-off" to fuel its propulsion unit. "What's boil-off?" I asked on the first day of this petroleum conference. I received the standard reply in such cases: "Don't worry about it, it's the same word in French." It took me a while — I had to ask three participants — but I eventually got my explanation: natural gas (methane) is liquefied for transport by ship (less volume means lower freight costs) and since the refrigeration facilities needed to keep the gas in liquid form are very expensive to operate, the liquid gas is cooled through natural evaporation of a part of the liquid. This part of the methane gas is then used as a fuel to propel the LNG tanker. Once I understood the sequence of events involved in boil-off, I could easily accept the use of the English term in French but was also able to use such terms as *évaporation*, *phase gazeuse*, *méthane* or *carburant*, according to context.

Specialists attending international conferences thus often fail to perceive the need for the interpreter to understand some of the basic principles of the subject at hand and believe that merely knowing the technical term is sufficient; yet knowing the technical term is generally of no help without some understanding of the processes involved.

Once, after a highly exacting meeting of bankers, I remember the Director of the French Caisse des Dépôts et Consignations saying that it seemed to him that the interpreter had actually understood and explained rather than translated. When I replied that his impression was correct, he decided that this could serve as a lesson in humility for those who, like himself, assumed that their sphere lay beyond the ken of ordinary mortals and was impenetrable to all but a chosen few. Although his remark was not the most graceful acknowledgement I have ever received, I took it as I believe it was intended, i.e., as a compliment.

Over the years, the interpreter's work leads him to delve into a diversity of subjects, to discover a vast range of human activities and to visit a wide variety of countries. His work brings him into contact with industrial cartels, labor unions, government officials and scientists. He is in a position to see, firsthand, the life styles and political philosophies of industrial countries and Third World nations. His work causes him to become interested in a whole range of subjects that would probably never have aroused his interest if he had not been a party to their discussion. It is a curious fact that, instead of diminishing interest, increased knowledge enhances it and that whenever interest is aroused new knowledge is acquired, as borne out by the fact that in the United States newspaper circulation increased enormously with the introduction of television newscasts. The interpreter who becomes interested in many of the subjects he deals with reads eclectically. Thus, even outside the conference hall, he is constantly acquiring new types of knowledge which he can link up with what he hears at conferences.

The interpreter's knowledge covers a wide range of disciplines and though it is acquired in a nonsystematic, somewhat random way (as he moves from one conference to another), it is solidly grounded because it has been mentally processed. Perhaps he never completely understands the inner workings of the processes whose end products he deals with. He is like the motorist who, without being a mechanic, can drive around the world if he so desires. Yet, in moving from one discipline to another, he encounters the same basic principles and his fragments of knowledge gradually blend into a coherent picture of people and life.

One may wonder how much longer interpreters will be able to continue in this manner, for increased specialization on the part of experts, along with more frequent contacts among them, could make their arguments too esoteric for the layman to understand, and this could conceivably compel interpreters to specialize and increase their knowledge in certain areas, while deliberately excluding others. Perhaps the time will come when the interpreter can no longer be an intelligent generalist, ready to work in any area of human activity, because the gap between his knowledge and that of the specialist will have widened to the point where nothing is comprehensible to him any more. This specialization would not mean that he would become an expert in certain selected fields, but that he would increase his knowledge more systematically in those fields, becoming specialized not only in the technique of interpretation but in certain subject areas as well, like a jeweler who confines his work to a few metals.

At present it is difficult to answer this question, but the interpreting profession may develop along these lines. When the profession still had only a few hundred members, conference interpreters were not inclined to specialize; however, since the number of conferences has increased, such a division of labor may become necessary. The interpreter would no longer find himself faced with a continually shifting kaleidoscopic picture, but would be able to concentrate on certain subjects about which he would be more knowledgeable.

If this were to occur, it would probably be even more difficult than it is today to find students capable of becoming interpreters, since − in addition to their natural aptitude for analysis, public speaking and languages − they would have to possess detailed knowledge of certain scientific or technical fields.

2. LANGUAGES

Although the participants at international conferences are more knowledgeable about their own fields than the interpreter, there is one area where his knowledge surpasses theirs, and that is, of course, the area of languages. His superior knowledge in this area is the very reason for his presence at conferences, not just as a linguist but also, because of his training and experience, as a specialist in oral communication.

Knowledge of several languages is generally the only quality that an interpreter is credited with, and if he is occasionally admired for anything, it is for his multilingualism. The reason we did not start by examining this problem of linguistic knowledge — as might have seemed natural — is because we felt it essential to first define what interpretation is. The preceding chapters will have shown that, while the existence of so many different languages explains the basic need for interpretation, languages are far from being the main source of difficulty in the practice of his profession. While the public at large believes that an interpreter's job consists of learning and using a lot of words in different languages, for the interpreter the problem of languages is only one component part of a much larger whole.

A careful distinction must thus be drawn between knowledge of languages, which is a prerequisite, and the use of languages in the technique of interpreting, which is a result of training.

For the interpreter, knowledge of languages is not an end in itself, but the essential prerequisite for interpretation, as we have tried to define it.

It is, however, far from easy to define what is meant by "knowing" a language. Few fields are so tainted with misconceptions, woolly thinking, wrong ideas and subjectivity. We shall therefore first attempt to define what knowledge of languages means for an interpreter, and then consider the purely linguistic problems that confront him as he applies his technique.

Classification of Working Languages

It is generally assumed that conference interpreters are multilingual and one of the standard questions they are always asked is "How many languages do you speak?" Their answer is invariably disappointing since, as a general rule, conference interpreters who are members of the International Association of Conference Interpreters rarely have more than three working languages. Not everyone is fortunate enough to spend his childhood in more than one country. Few of those who have a "gift" for languages, in other words the gift of being able to keep them apart, also possess the qualities necessary to be able to interpret. Yet even if they do, that alone would not be sufficient because their languages have to be among the world's most widely spoken, virtually the only languages used at international conferences in the western world. The following languages have traditionally been used among European and international organizations: English, French, Russian, German, Spanish, Italian, and Dutch, with Arabic being added later. Other languages are sometimes used for bilateral meetings but may not require interpretation. The entry of Finland and Norway into the European Union will create a new demand for interpreters. However, the problems that various languages pose in interpretation are no different from those posed by the traditional conference languages.

The International Association of Conference Interpreters has established language classification standards for its members. The interpreter's first language, termed his "A" language, should be a real mother tongue. AIIC thereby discourages those who, in the jargon of the profession, are called "alingual," that is people who speak several languages, each of which interferes with the others. Alinguals originate from areas where several languages are spoken and not kept strictly separate. Alternatively, they have had a native language but have, in part, forgotten it during their stay in another country, without acquiring full command of the second language. AIIC has, however, recognized some cases of true bilingualism; these are people who lived in two different countries as children, pursued their secondary and higher education alternately in both countries and have, on top of this fortunate set of circumstances, consciously striven to keep their languages separate.[2]

The second category established by AIIC is the "B" language — a language of which the interpreter has a perfect knowledge but which cannot, however, be considered as a native language. It is possible for an interpreter to work successfully into his "B" language in consecutive interpretation, since he has sufficient time to restructure the message to be communicated. However, this does not hold true for simultaneous interpretation, because here the interpreter

---

[2]In 1994, AIIC had over 2,000 members, 241 of whom were bilinguals (two "A" languages).

must have a total feel for the language so that the expressions he uses will sound immediately familiar to his listeners, leaving them free to concentrate on the content of the message. Years of experience in the profession, a thorough study of the relevant terminology beforehand and a broad experience of interpreting will, however, enable an interpreter to do a respectable job of interpreting, into his "B" language, technical material that includes a great many words that can be translated literally. However, the interpreter must have exceptional flair, intelligence and experience if he is to render an explanation clearly enough so that the occasional less than perfect phrasing can be overlooked.

Finally there is the "C" or passive language, a language that the interpreter must *understand perfectly*. Only after living for extended periods in a country where this language is spoken can he acquire the degree of knowledge necessary to be able to claim it as a "C" language. Nevertheless, with this language the emphasis is not on proficiency in expression but on understanding the meaning of words, turns of phrase and idiomatic expressions.

The reader should now be familiar with the language requirements of the profession. However, this information is probably not sufficient and there are undoubtedly a number of questions that remain unanswered. We shall now address these questions.

Knowing Languages

The languages used in interpretation today are nothing if not contemporary. Older forms of today's languages, which are the subject of philological and literary study, are not used in interpretation and neither are the thousands of languages and dialects of regional importance only which exist throughout the world.

To get some idea of how rich these languages are today, let us look at the number of words they contain. The ten-volume Larousse dictionary boasts 450,000 entries which correspond to at least as many definitions, if not words. The Encyclopaedia Britannica lists 600,000 terms.

To realize how much of any one language is normally used at international conferences today, one must exclude archaic words and connotations that are no longer used except in literature, but include all those that have become an integral part of the language in other ways: proper names, acronyms, brand names and trademarks, titles of books and films, company names, etc. all of which are proliferating wildly.

Let us take the case of proper names. What is said about a Mr. Dupont can take on a very different meaning depending on whether he is an American, a Frenchman or the Secretary-General of the organization. In interpretation, a proper name thus has a meaning and for the interpreter it is just as much a part of the language as any other word. He must be just as aware of these words as he is of the more usual words and phrases.

Although the 450,000 and 600,000 definitions mentioned above serve as a handy illustration of the richness of languages, in point of fact the vocabulary of any language is infinite. With this in mind, it is interesting to compare the size of vocabulary different individuals may possess in their native languages; from the peasant who can express the routine activities of his everyday life in two or three thousand words, to the poet who has a vocabulary that is probably ten times greater. And when one considers the total body of words used in all their different meanings, it is probably ten times greater than the vocabulary of the poet.

Nothing is more difficult than defining linguistic knowledge. What does it mean to "know" a language? A language is not a finite or clearly defined mass, which you either possess in its entirety or not at all. You do not "know" a language in the same way you know a theorem or poem by heart. You can only know it more or less thoroughly. Some speak two languages with perfect ease, yet have a very limited vocabulary in both. Conversely, philologists or authorities on theoretical linguistics, for example, who do not study languages for the purpose of speaking them, may have a very thorough knowledge of the languages they study, but would be unable to use them to communicate. Their knowledge is thus also limited.

Anyone who has to deal with the realities of today's world has some knowledge, however minimal, of a foreign language, either because his job requires it or because he comes from a country where the language is not widely spoken beyond that country's borders (the Dutch, the Swedes, the Poles and, increasingly, the French are finding themselves forced to learn another language). But neither the scholar with his literary or theoretical knowledge nor the expert with his specialized knowledge, nor the polyglot can be considered to have an exhaustive knowledge of the language, but merely a working knowledge.

Acquiring a foreign language is so difficult that few specialists in linguistics are at the same time practicing linguists. It is worth noting that although any child, regardless of his intelligence, learns a language by picking up what he hears around him, it is extremely rare for an adult to do so. Yet perfect command of two or three languages is an absolute must for anyone who wants to learn how to interpret.

Knowledge of Languages as a Prerequisite

An interpreter must know his languages thoroughly before he begins to practice the profession, because he cannot learn or improve his knowledge of a language while expressing the meaning of a message at 150 words a minute.

Nevertheless there is a tendency to base training courses for interpreters on the techniques used for teaching translation, which involves converting the words of one language into those of another and is therefore a language-learning exercise at the same time. Many schools claim to teach both language and interpretation at the same time. But language-learning exercises can only impede the learning of interpretation because the evanescence of the spoken language and the interpreter's concentration on the meaning of what is being said are not conducive to language learning. This is why we contend that, in order to learn how to interpret, the would-be interpreter must already have acquired a command of his language that we would describe as perfect, if the phrase "perfect command of a language" were not already overused. The interpreter's "working knowledge" of a language must satisfy a substantial number of criteria. He must be able to understand the spoken language on first hearing, he must be intuitive and articulate and possess a wide vocabulary. Furthermore, he must have acquired command of the foreign language at an early age and then followed this with studies at foreign schools or universities. He must also have a knack for communicating.

The interpreter is neither a philologist nor a polyglot, but he must be able to apply his very broad and specific linguistic knowledge to a great many fields. It is to this linguistic knowledge that he will add the extra vocabulary acquired throughout his working life. (A language has an infinite number of words and the interpreter should be constantly adding to his vocabulary.)

It is also throughout his working life that the interpreter gradually learns to understand the infinite variety of accents he hears. However many years one has spent abroad, it is impossible to have lived in all the English-speaking countries of the world (from the United States to Ghana to Australia, not to mention specific areas like Texas and Yorkshire) and to understand every possible accent. It is just as impossible to know every language, and yet it would be useful to be able to recognize Swedish turns of phrase when they pop up in English or hispanicisms that creep into the French of a delegate forced by the conference's rules to speak a language that is not his own. The interpreter's ear does gradually become accustomed to this phenomenon and he ends up understanding much better than other participants the English spoken by Indians or Japanese, for example. If he is to get used to this great variety of accents, the interpreter must have an exceptional understanding of the spoken language before he begins to practice the profession.

The interpreter works with language that he hears once only. He must be able to make out the sounds of a language he hears at a conference accurately and effortlessly so that he can identify the words he hears regardless of the voice quality or intonation of the speaker. His auditory perception of the foreign language should be almost comparable to that of a native speaker. It is particularly important that the conference interpreter have this ability, because he is constantly coming into contact with terms that are not used in everyday conversation, and it is a fact that the less a word is used, the more difficult it is for the ear to make it out. This problem is exacerbated in simultaneous interpretation, because the electronic equipment alters the quality of the sound and the interpreter's perception of it.

In this respect, the interpreter is different from other linguists who work with the written word and who do not encounter similar problems, since all writing is in the form of printed symbols. The problem of deciphering individual handwriting has long since disappeared, whereas the problem of understanding different pronunciations still persists, for the interpreter, in a very real way.

What is true with respect to the passive knowledge of one or more languages is even truer when these languages are to be used actively. One has to learn a language at a very early age to pronounce it like a native. Of course, a person with an ear for languages can sometimes pass for a native speaker, but once he finds himself in the shoes of an interpreter, where he must be able to express the most subtle shades of meaning, his native-like fluency soon disappears. His words no longer flow easily and naturally, and his pronunciation and vocabulary reflect the influence of his native language. We will return to this point later on to underscore the importance of using one's native language as the target language in interpretation.

Knowing a language also means knowing its *structure*. A language is not only the sum total of its words, it also represents a frame of mind, a way of looking at the world. Knowing a language means having a feel for its structure, so that it is possible to understand a message by following its internal logic, even when a specific word has been missed.

This feel for a language must be as deeply rooted in the interpreter as his ability to recognize its sound and grasp intuitively the meaning of everything that is said.

Most conference interpreters have actually lived in more than one country and have learned at least one of their "foreign" languages during childhood.

This innate knowledge of a language, this intuitive feel for its oral expression, forms the basis for the interpreter's never-ending acquisition of vocabulary in that language.

Languages and Words

The sum total of lexical items that an interpreter knows in each of his languages is considerable. He is not called upon to express the experiences of daily life using a relatively small number of expressions, like the bilingual inhabitants of border areas whom we mentioned earlier, or the tour guide, or the hotel porter. Throughout his professional career the interpreter explores all areas of human knowledge.

Therefore, he must be able to tap, in each of his working languages (active and passive), a wealth of vocabulary that is at least comparable to that of an educated native speaker. This does not imply that he should know so many lexical items in each of his working languages that he turns into a multilingual human dictionary or a walking encyclopedia. We shall see shortly that there are relatively few words that stump the interpreter to the point where he cannot derive some meaning out of them in a given context.

A language is made up of words only a few of which are part and parcel of the everyday vocabulary of those who use that language as a medium of expression. On top of this core of everyday words (which enable us to say that all the inhabitants of a given country speak the same language) there are thousands of other words or word meanings that are used for communication within subgroups, such as members of the same family, profession, etc.

This does not mean, however, that such words are incomprehensible to someone who speaks the same language but is not a member of the group, since these words are, to a great extent, drawn from everyday language, and so it is easy to understand the new meaning a term may have by associating it with its primary meaning. For instance the shape of a new object may be similar to the shape of an object that already has a name: the word *grenade* in French (the name of the fruit "pomegranate") was extended to mean the weapon. The function that an object serves can call to mind a similar function in another field of activity. For example, the word "jacket," an item that covers a part of the body, has been extended to create the term "water jacket" for the outer casing of a cylinder or pipe. Specialized terminology is also made up of terms borrowed from foreign languages or created from etymological roots. "Sputnik" and "cybernetic" are but two examples.

Specialized terminology used by one group is quite likely to be taken up by others as well. A great deal of cross-utilization goes on and certain specialized terms in one language often turn up in another with similar or identical meaning. The interpreter does not necessarily have to know these terms beforehand in order to be able to understand them when he hears them during a conference.

There is a difference then between these words which the interpreter knows to the extent of being able to give an exact definition of each of their meanings and those whose new meaning he uncovers by association. Once he has become aware of this new meaning it becomes either a temporary or permanent part of his knowledge, often without his realizing at what point he first acquired it. Let us take the word *fonçage* ("drilling") for example, and let us assume the interpreter is not familiar with it. If this word were to appear in a context where its meaning were clear, such as in *le fonçage du puits no. 1 de la mine durera quinze mois*,[3] the interpreter who did not know this word would probably not distinguish it very clearly when he heard it and it probably would not stick in his mind. He would, however, render the meaning of the sentence without realizing that it contained an unfamiliar word — at least in simultaneous. I remember once, while interpreting simultaneously into French, hearing the English word "chivvy," which I did not know, and coming out with the word *éperonner* even though when I initially heard the English word I had the impression that I had heard an unfamiliar word. A colleague who noticed my slight hesitation told me afterwards that I had indeed rendered the exact meaning of this word previously unknown to me. If, on the other hand, a new word crops up frequently at a given meeting it becomes more distinct in the interpreter's mind and, by hearing it in context during the course of the discussion, he seeks to clarify its meaning and determine whether his initial impression was right or not. But for the interpreter to acquire a clear understanding of the process, the machinery and the equipment involved in a *fonçage*, the word must be used at many meetings and in many different contexts; although he understood the new term when he first heard it, he needs to hear it in a number of contexts for it to be thoroughly learned and digested and become an integral part of his background knowledge.

Up to this point we have confined our discussion to vocabulary acquisition in one single language; in this respect the interpreter differs from speakers who share his own mother tongue only in that he has more frequent contact with words and word meanings that are not commonly used. Any area of human activity can be the subject

---

[3]"The drilling of mine shaft No. 1 will take 15 months."

71

of an international meeting and for each one slightly different terms are used. The interpreter acquires a vocabulary that is greater and certainly more diverse than that of his fellow citizens.

We cannot continue to examine the problems that unfamiliar words pose for the interpreter without looking at his second language (to simplify matters we will disregard the third language that a conference interpreter usually knows). There are instances where context alone will not help an interpreter understand a term or expression he hears in one language, but where its equivalent in the other language often provides an additional "context" which helps clarify what would otherwise have remained unclear. As we said earlier, every word evokes a semantic field. Corresponding expressions in two languages evoke slightly different semantic fields in each, and these tend to complement each other. Take the example of "virgin copper" in English. The French term *cuivre de première fusion* clarifies and explains the English term, and vice versa.

Yet it would be incorrect to think that an interpreter will come across very many words with which he is unfamiliar in a conference, or that these terms will be numerous enough to constitute an obstacle to his understanding of the message. It should be borne in mind that while the sum total of words in any language is enormous compared to the vocabulary any one individual may possess, the interpreter never has to deal with the entire language at any one time. At each conference he hears a limited number of words which constitute a minute part of the total lexicon of the language. It is this limited vocabulary that contains the words and expressions whose meaning he has to figure out.

The number of new words and expressions the interpreter will come across in any given conference will depend on his experience and on the type of conference, but they rarely exceed a few dozen, so they are not too numerous to learn. Only rarely will an interpreter hear a word that is totally unknown to him and which he cannot understand either by referring to its etymology or by deducing its meaning from the context.

From One Language to Another

We began this book by pointing out that interpreting could never consist of a mere word-for-word translation from one language to another and that, between the time the interpreter hears a message and the time he re-expresses it in another language, he must have carried out the essential process of analyzing its meaning. This being said, the interpreter is still left with the task of taking one verbal statement and expressing it verbally in another language, a process which necessarily involves some translation or, if you will, a search for *equivalents* in two different languages.

In preceding chapters we warned against the all too commonly held belief that interpretation is a mere transfer of words from one language to another and we emphasized the fact that, in view of the speed with which interpretation takes place, such a process would be inconceivable and could only end in failure. But there are other reasons, which have to do with the very nature of languages, why word-for-word translation from one language to another is impossible.

We have shown what a *working knowledge* of languages involves for an interpreter. Let us now see if words truly can match up across languages, if they can be fitted together like pieces in a jigsaw puzzle, in other words, if having the same knowledge in two different languages and substituting a word in one language for a word in another is sufficient to overcome the language barrier.

It would not be true to say that this cannot be done at all. There are words that have direct equivalents in other languages, just as there are words that are "untranslatable." This is a cliché which, for once, is true, but with one small correction: untranslatable words are the rule, and words that always have exact translations the exception. To put it more clearly, we shall make a distinction between two concepts that are often confused when people speak of "untranslatable" words: the concept of *translating* in the sense of transcoding from one language to another by substituting one word for another, and that of *expressing* the same thing in two languages.

Words like "sun," "father," "love" and "death" can be translated. These are words that flow from basic human experience that transcends societies and the language they speak. But human experience is as varied as the civilizations that man has created, so that civilizations differ not only because of their languages but also because of their specific ideas and objects.

Is "bread" really the equivalent of French *pain*? To Americans bread is a spongy substance cut up in slices and wrapped in plastic. To the French, bread is a long, golden crusty loaf. There is no need to go as far as words like *Gemüt* and *Schadenfreude* to maintain that some words are untranslatable. We would contend that *virtually all words are untranslatable*, if we define as translatable words that have an exact equivalent in another language and that retain this exact equivalency regardless of context. It is this belief in translatability that gives rise to questions like "How do you say such and such a word in German or French?" Such translatability, we maintain, does not exist for the vast majority of a language's vocabulary, with a few specific exceptions: numbers, for instance, to take an example that springs immediately to mind. To translate words as one translates numbers, however, would be tantamount to speaking as people in bilingual areas speak, where languages have, to a great extent, lost their structural specificities and one comes across expressions such as the French-Canadian *Vous êtes bienvenu* based on the English "You are welcome"[4] or the Swiss expression *expédition par adresse* modeled on the German *Adressenversand*.[5] This is only natural since the spoken language is the means of expression of both individual and collective thinking within a society; it is difficult for an individual living in that society to keep on saying the same thing in two different ways. In bilingual areas this means that the two languages have become so similar to each other that they differ only in vocabulary. It would be more accurate in such cases to speak of "bivocabularism" rather than bilingualism.

For participants at international conferences whose languages reflect entirely different ways of structuring their thought, such a word-for-word translation would probably be incomprehensible. For people who really are "foreigners," a statement made in one language has to be restructured before being expressed in another, and in

---

[4]Normally *à votre service*.

[5]Normally *distribution de journaux aux abonnés* ("delivery of newspapers by mail").

order to accomplish this the interpreter has to fall back on the semantic content of the information on which the statement was based.

Suppose one could move from one language to another by using simple word-for-word translation without relying on the intelligence of the person "translating." This would be tantamount to admitting that languages have an objective existence of their own, that they function independently and that the form of the message and the information conveyed are identical.

This could never be the case, because the meaning of the vast majority of words is derived just as much, if not more, from the context in which they appear as from their primary meaning. Furthermore, the number of equivalents that a word has in another language is just as great as the number of meanings it acquires with changing contexts. Restating a message in another language requires constant creativity; *here we find ourselves moving imperceptibly from the notion of translation to that of expression.* Each time the context shifts, the same word takes on a slightly different meaning which must almost invariably be rendered by a different word in the target language. Therefore, it is no longer a question of knowing the lexical equivalents of words in two different languages that can serve as automatic substitutes for one another, but of finding terms that will express "the same thing" regardless of the words used in the original statement. We shall define those words for which new equivalents must constantly be found as "contextual"; they deserve this name, because they match the original terms but cannot be called translations of them, since the match is not based on the word itself, but on the object or concept that the word describes. On this premise, everything that is said in one language can be expressed in another, provided that the two languages belong to societies that have attained comparable levels of development.

When an object or a concept exists in a given cultural milieu there is a way for it to be expressed in another language, as long as one does not set out to translate the words but to express the idea. When he hears a knock at his door, a Serb will say *slobodno*, a Frenchman *entrez*, a German *herein*, and an Englishman "come in," and each finds the correct way to say what he means by taking stock of the situation in which he finds himself and not by referring to an equivalent phrase in another language. Translated into English, *slobodno* would be "free," *herein* would be "into here" and only the French would be a translation for "come in." The entire theory of interpretation can be based on the principle that this simple example illustrates. *Interpretation is, to a great extent, the verbal expression of things and ideas accompanied by the non-deliberate creation of temporary linguistic equivalents.* The only reason certain words are thought to be untranslatable is because the concepts that they express are expressed in a different way in another language. In point of fact, what is lacking is not a way of expressing certain ideas, but words with an identical semantic range in any two languages, and exact lexical equivalents that would remain consistent in meaning, regardless of context. Words, i.e., the concepts they represent, are "untranslatable" only when their referent does not yet exist in the society using the target language. It is impossible to express something that does not exist!

In this situation, since translating or restating is impossible, it is more a matter of introducing a new concept into an existing cultural framework, i.e., developing it through explanation before formally introducing it into the other language by giving it a name. The foreign word might be preserved intact, as has been done with "dacha" from Russian or *software* in French, which comes from computers, or a new word will be created as was done with "cybernetic," or a new meaning is given to an old word as in the case of "satellite" which very quickly lost its adjective "artificial."

Translation of Translatable Words

In Chapter IV "Expression," we shall see how the message is transmitted independently of the words that convey it. Although we have stated that most words are not translatable, we should examine those words that, in interpretation, are "translatable" when, in a given context and for a given meaning, they have an equivalent in another language.

A language is not divided into "translatable" and "contextual" words. Words that are translatable in one situation become contextual in another, and vice versa. Even the archetype of the translatable word, the number, can be one or the other. For example, the numeral *quinze* ("15") is translatable when it corresponds to "fifteen" in English or *fünfzehn* in German, but it becomes contextual when the expression *quinze jours* is equivalent to "a fortnight" or *vierzehn Tage*. Let us look at a few examples: "emergency" in English is a contextual word, yet "emergency exit" translates perfectly well into French as *sortie de secours*. The word "river" can be translated, according to the context, by *fleuve*, *rivière* or *cours d'eau*, but it becomes contextual in the phrase "The dam built on the Indus River," where "river" would be omitted in French: *Le barrage construit sur l'Indus*. Another example would be the rendering of "We shall have lunch on the river," by *Nous mangerons sur le bateau*.

It is interesting to take a closer look at what happens to translatable words in interpretation and examine their ready equivalents in two languages. We have seen that a certain number of words (sun, father, love, death, etc.), which all draw on basic human experience, have equivalents in other languages. We shall term the translation of such words "etymological" translation, since it is valid in rendering the primary meaning of the word as given in the dictionary, i.e., "father" in English is translated by *père* in French and *Vater* in German, etc. This "etymological" translation no longer works, however, as soon as a word takes on a meaning different from its primary meaning.

While the German word *Mutter* has a primary equivalent in "mother," *mère*, etc., in the word *Schraubenmutter* ("threaded nut") it must be rendered in French by *matrice* and even *écrou*, and by "placenta" in the word *Mutterkuchen*. We shall term this type of translation "conventional" translation. Because experts have attempted to devise a terminology for their respective fields such that a given term clearly stands for a particular object or concept and will not cause confusion, there are countless words that have conventional (i.e., agreed) equivalents in other languages.

Increasingly, organizations that regularly hold international conferences are appointing terminology committees which draw up parallel lists of words in the various fields and languages covered by the organization. Although it would be dangerous to presume that an equivalent found by one terminology committee will necessarily be valid in a multitude of different contexts, these conventional equivalents are of considerable importance for interpretation. Words that have been identified as equivalents of words in other languages become like proper names for precisely defined objects or concepts.

And because of this they will always have the same equivalent in another language in a given context.

These in-house glossaries, reflecting agreements reached among experts of the same organization and drawn up for their own use, are more valuable to the interpreter than so-called technical dictionaries, which contain definitions that are for the most part too broad and equivalents that are too etymological. Whether one is dealing with a Committee for the Standardization of Gas Appliances or an International Railway Conference discussing the introduction of automatic coupling, the glossary drawn up by the terminology committee of the organization will be the most likely source of exact equivalents for the target language.

Let us consider the example of the English term "calorific value." The French interpreter's immediate reaction would be to translate the primary meaning of both words and to say *valeur calorifique*. The French experts on the terminology committee, however, who did not refer to the English term but to their understanding of what the "thing" is and the way they express it in French, put forward the expression *pouvoir calorifique*, which has become the conventional equivalent of "calorific value." To draw up the glossary all they have to do is list "calorific value" side by side with *pouvoir calorifique*.

An etymological translation — rendering the primary meaning of a word — is not therefore always a useful translation, and indeed is seldom so at international conferences. What we mean by a "translatable" word is one for which not only the primary meaning is translatable but also for which a number of equivalents can be found in another language — equivalents which are often far removed from the primary meaning.

Here are a few examples: *kalkulatorischer Wert* is *valeur actualisée* in French and not *valeur calculée*,[6] and "seller's market" is *marché fort* and not *marché de vendeurs*.

Dictionaries often have the irritating habit of only doing the job halfway. They list the terms used in a language but instead of drawing up separate lists in various languages and then matching them up, they translate the words' primary meanings and leave it at

---

[6]"present value" in English.

that. What is more, such multilingual dictionaries usually only list words that are supposed to correspond to other words without defining them by providing precise descriptions of the designated objects or equivalent concepts, and they fail to sufficiently delimit their usage.

In interpreting translatable words, the interpreter, who must make himself understood and who thus speaks the language of his listeners as they are accustomed to hearing it, does not translate the primary meaning of words but supplies the equivalent meaning in the target language. For these words therefore he does not seek to devise new equivalents, valid only for that particular context (as with contextual words), nor does he resort to an etymological translation since that would only help him render the primary meaning. Rather, he relies on the automatic process of conventional translation which he has developed through learning and memorization, and which causes him to retrieve the correct term as soon as he hears its equivalent.

Thus we see that there are three types of equivalence in translation: *etymological translation*, which translates the primary meaning of the word; *conventional translation*, which supplies set terms for words used in a given field; and *contextual translation*, which is the creative restatement of an idea using semantic equivalents which are valid only in a given context.

As long as translation machines are unable to make the distinction between these three types of equivalence, the service they can provide is likely to remain very limited.

Specialized Terminology

To get into the habit of conventional translation, the interpreter must continually learn new terminology. For every international conference, he is forced to supplement his knowledge by acquiring additional vocabulary. This is an ongoing, never-ending process. Prior to a conference, the interpreter consults encyclopedias which, together with the glossaries published by the organizations, are his sources of terminology. It is here that he sees the words placed in a meaningful context. Of course, he only finds them in one language at a time, but he can identify many valuable equivalents by first consulting an American encyclopedia, and then a French one, and reading the articles they contain on the subject in question.

However valuable these glossaries and encyclopedias are, they remain tools prepared for purposes other than interpreting. Glossaries enable a specialist to read a text in its original language or a translator to find the terms he needs. Encyclopedias are written for the general public. Neither the glossary nor the encyclopedia relieves the interpreter of the need to lift vocabulary from the conference's working documents or note the terms used by the speakers in a discussion. The conference documents provide the interpreter with the most useful source of vocabulary in the two languages. They include papers prepared separately by French and American engineers working on the same subject, and reports of previous conferences held by the same organization. The interpreter who will be working into French begins by reading the documents distributed to the French-speaking participants. Once he has a good grasp of the French terms as they are used in context, once he knows for instance that a French dam designer will say *tractions dans le béton* and *continuité de profil*, he turns to the English documents to match up his newly acquired French terms with the correct English ones. He finds that the English term "structure" is *ouvrage* in French and "spillway" is *évacuateur de crues*; that "backwater sloughing" in English is *érosion régressive* in French. He learns these equivalences and uses them in his work. Elsewhere he will learn that to Texan peanut growers "peas" more often mean peanuts than green peas, and that "to brood" in American agricultural extension parlance means to tend the newly hatched chicks as well as just hatching the eggs. Or, again, he will find that to French specialists in a certain field "wire" is not *fil de fer* but *toile métallique*.

This ongoing acquisition of vocabulary by the interpreter is accompanied by an acute awareness that certain word meanings are valid only for a specific conference. Word meanings can vary not only from one industry to another (the term *roulement*[7] is to be translated into German as *Kugellager* in the context of a steel mill and as *Wälzlager* in the manufacture of nuts and bolts), but also within the same industry (depending on the region, the French will

---

[7]"ball bearing."

say *ferraille*, where the Belgians say *mitraille*, while *bocage* is used for "scrap iron" in the eastern part of France only).

This is all well and good. Yet it is obvious that the interpreter cannot restrict himself to learning words and their equivalents without seeking to find out what they express. Learning that the French equivalent of the English word "spigot" is *buse* will not mean much, in the absence of any background knowledge. An interpreter usually acquires new vocabulary by first realizing that he does not know a term in his own language, finding out what it means, and then looking for a suitable equivalent in the other language.

When he knows the terminology in his own language, the interpreter studies the documents in the foreign language from which he will be interpreting ("B" language or "C" language); in doing so, he identifies the correct equivalent terms in both languages. This exercise may well cause him to look more closely at certain words in his own language that he may have glossed over because of their apparent familiarity. He may have glossed over the word *sous-pression*, for example, in a document on dams. However, when he sees the word "uplift" in English he realizes that *sous-pression* is a type of pressure that is exerted at the base of a dam, and not one that is lower than average, as he might at first have thought.

Yet the question often asked of interpreters is still quite logical: "What does an interpreter do when he hears a technical word he does not know?" This is actually two questions in one, for the interpreter might not know what the word *means*, or he might not know how to translate it. It may happen that he knows neither because, however broad his experience, an interpreter can always be caught unawares by words that crop up unexpectedly during a conference. If he comes across a word whose meaning he does not know during consecutive interpretation, he can always ask those attending the meeting. In simultaneous he can repeat it phonetically (technical experts often know the technical terms in the other language) for want of understanding its meaning and hearing the right equivalent. This is where the interpreter has an unquestionable advantage over the translator, in that he has direct access to a precious source of information: experts discussing their subject in two different languages.

Let us consider an example. In a conference on shipping where the discussion centered on dikes at the mouth of the harbor, one part of the dike was called *risberme* in French. This word was completely unknown to the French interpreter and, struck by it, he jotted it down and attempted to understand its meaning during the remainder of the French speech, with the aid of the accompanying slides, glossaries at hand, etc. He was thus prepared to use the French term *risberme* when he later heard the word "shoulder" in a speech he had to interpret from English.

The interpreter rarely encounters words of this kind which are completely unknown to him and, even if he does, they pose little danger because upon hearing them he realizes he does not know them and rapidly tries to find out what they mean.

Words that the interpreter thinks he knows, but does not, are much more dangerous. The problem of *risberme* in French is easier to solve than that of "shoulder" heard in the same context in English. With *risberme* one's immediate reaction is to try to determine the meaning of the word, and then find the English equivalent; upon hearing the word "shoulder" in English, on the other hand, one's initial reaction might be to translate it by *épaule* and leave it at that. The interpreter, however, in constant contact with the living language, is by nature always suspicious of etymological translations. When he hears the words *risberme* being used by French-speaking participants it does not take him long to associate it with "shoulder" in English.

It is much more common for the interpreter to encounter a word he knows, or at least whose meaning he understands, but whose equivalent momentarily escapes him.

Let us consider the example of an interpreter interpreting into English. He hears a German speaker say *Eiweiss* and for some reason or another the word "protein" does not immediately come to mind. He wryly rejects "egg white" and settles on "albumin," for want of a better word. The German speaker is followed by an English speaker who has understood the interpreter and himself uses the word "protein." The English interpreter, who can take a break while English speakers are talking, listens and notes the words they are using. When he hears "protein" he knows immediately that this was the word he was looking for.

Interpreters take many notes in the booth. Some may seem rather elementary because they are not of a technical nature; they are, however, important because they enable the interpreter to express himself with greater accuracy. The interpreter hears the French speakers say *traiter un terrain à l'insecticide* where the English would say "to spread an insecticide"; he jots this down for future use. I remember having the word *député* written on a piece of paper which I kept in front of me for entire sessions of the Consultative Assembly of the Council of Europe so that I would not slip up and say *membre du Parlement* for "Member of Parliament," which kept coming through my earphones.

Being aware of the limits to his knowledge, the interpreter not only notes words that are totally new to him but, when dealing with areas where he lacks expert knowledge, approaches all words with a certain suspicion, because any one of them could have a meaning of which he is unaware. It is precisely because he is aware of his limited knowledge, even of his native language, that he is able to overcome the difficulties caused by terms he comes across when dealing with unfamiliar subjects.

The fact that there are words for which equivalents must be found in another language forces the interpreter to prepare for conferences, and remain very alert during meetings, in order to pick up the terms that will enable him to find the correct equivalents. By the same token, the very existence of these "translatable" expressions considerably lightens his task, since once he knows them he no longer has to *interpret* them, in the sense of restating them by disregarding the original wording, as he must for most of the message of which these words are a part. The fact that "translatable" expressions come to mind in a manner that is virtually automatic, after a few hours work, greatly relieves the stress under which an interpreter works.

CHAPTER IV

EXPRESSION

1. THE DISSOCIATION OF LANGUAGE AND THOUGHT

We have seen that, if he is to understand the speaker, the interpreter must have an exceptional command of the source language and sufficient knowledge of the subject matter. Because he is in the same meeting as both speaker and listener, he knows in what capacity the speaker is speaking and understands the purpose of each of his statements. He then uses that knowledge to analyze and understand the speaker's words. Let us now examine how the interpreter expresses what he has understood in order to *make himself understood in turn*.

Having gone through the process that we outlined earlier, the interpreter finds himself, by the time he is ready to speak, in the same position as anybody speaking spontaneously. Being in possession of a thought which, at that moment, commands all his attention, he expresses it in his native language following the normal pattern of the speech process. The better the interpreter understands the speaker's thought, the more it becomes his own thought and the more the three steps involved in interpretation (listening, understanding and expression) appear to blend into two (listening and expression), which is what causes the mildly attentive listener to think he is hearing a literal translation.

However, it is comprehension — the intermediate step in the interpretative process, after listening and before expression — which is responsible for the speed at which the message is rendered. Comprehension also involves the most important part of interpretation: the shedding of the verbal form which conveys the speaker's message and the subsequent appearance of the interpreter's thought in its place. This causes the message to revert to a non-verbal state similar to that in which it existed prior to being uttered by the speaker. It can then be re-expressed by the interpreter at the normal speed of speech.

The difference between these two thoughts is that the interpreter's is far more highly structured than was the speaker's initial thought. Indeed, any initial non-verbal thought remains intuitive to a great extent and does not really become clear until it is completely formed through a process of constant feedback, in which one statement influences the next, enabling the idea to develop, and thereby clarifying the concept.

The same process, in which thought is monitored by language, is at work while the interpreter is rendering the message. However, he does not use this process to elaborate on the concept further, because it is already explicit enough when he receives it; rather, he uses the process to express the speaker's thought as clearly as he can and often manages to express it more clearly than the speaker did himself. The speaker concentrates on clarifying his idea and expressing it appropriately. The interpreter is spared the first task since the thought is conveyed to him in its final form. He can thus concentrate on expressing that thought and on choosing the terms that he feels will most effectively convey it.

Theoretically, there is no reason why the interpreter's version of the thought, as it is the spontaneous expression of an idea, should show any trace of having been originally stated in another language. *In other words, what the interpreter says is, in principle, independent of the source language.*

The idea that thought can be dissociated from its verbal form may come as a surprise to those who have lived in a monolingual environment and have always felt the two were one and the same. When a child learns to talk, he learns to express in his native language the feelings he experiences which were there before he learned to talk, but which he very quickly learns to identify with the words used to describe them. He then learns to formulate concepts, put together from the words used to convey the thoughts of those around him. Thus it is through language that we come into full possession of our thought, develop it and clarify it, and take it beyond the level of feelings to that of concepts. The frequent tendency to consider *speaking* and *thinking* as one and the same stems from the fact that human thought could never have existed in all its complexity without language's ability to express the finest shades of meaning. This does not mean that language and thought are one and the same, but that there is a constant two-way flow whereby mental impulses are converted into language and language is reduced to mental impulses.

The interpreter who is experienced in expressing his thoughts in different languages realizes the futility of the question he is often asked: "What language do you think in?" He senses that thought has no verbal structure before it is formulated and that once it has been developed and clarified by language it reverts to a non-verbal state in the human brain. He knows that human knowledge and experience are not stored in the brain in verbal form and is aware of the constant two-way flow between linguistic encoding (language) and the non-verbal manipulating of concepts (thought), realizing that it is a unique characteristic of the mind of *Homo sapiens*.

2. NATIVE LANGUAGE AND INTERFERENCE

The process of linguistic encoding is spontaneous with an adult speaking his native language. This is a natural advantage that the interpreter exploits to the full by choosing to express himself in his native language and applying his analytical skills to his second or acquired language.

There are interpreters who can do both equally spontaneously in two languages. These are the true bilinguals, who are few and far between and who are the exceptions that prove the rule that simultaneous interpretation can only be done properly into one's native language. There are certain types of speeches that can be interpreted into the interpreter's second language in consecutive. Basically, however, it is the spontaneity of the native language that is responsible for the speed at which a message can be retransmitted, as well as for the clarity of its interpreted form.

The problem of communication, i.e., mutual comprehension, is considerable enough when it takes place between persons of the same culture. How much more difficult it is then to make a speaker understood by his listeners when they come from different cultures, are accustomed to different ways of thinking and have different cultural frames of reference. Yet this is the job of the interpreter since, by definition, he is there to bring about this mutual comprehension between people who are unfamiliar with each other's language and also, to a greater or lesser extent, with each other's cultures.

He manages to accomplish this task primarily because the spontaneity of his native language provides him with the ability to adapt to his listeners, thereby ensuring that they understand what he is saying to them.

The world offers many examples of different types of languages that enable information to be clearly transmitted if the usual system of communication is not available. I remember for instance a young Greek girl whom I met while vacationing who managed to make us understand that the young girl with her was her twin sister. She supplemented a torrent of incomprehensible words with gestures, using two fingers to point alternately to herself and her sister, and then finally placed her hand on her stomach until we understood that they had once been together in the same womb. This example involves the communicating of a very simple piece of information, but the interpreter does very much the same thing when he carries an idea from its conceptual state to its verbal expression. Stimulated solely by the concept itself and impelled by the clarity of the idea which has become his own, the interpreter creates a verbal expression that is totally faithful to the original meaning. This meaning is first expressed by the speaker who, given the context in which he finds himself, does not have an infinite range of synonymous words or phrases from which to choose. The interpreter, in expressing what is now his own thought and forgetting the speaker's words while absorbing the message in its entirety, is just as limited in his choice of words because there are only so many different ways to express a certain idea in a given context. What the interpreter says not only conforms to the meaning of the original statement, but also reflects the style of the original which bears the stamp of the speaker's personality.

When an interpreter interpreting into French knows what "processed cheese" is, either because he has eaten it or has watched it being made, and has a good command of his native language, the expression *fromage cuit* automatically comes to him without the possible translations of the verb "to process" (*transformer, traiter*, etc.) popping up to interfere with the interpretation. Instead of seeking to associate the verb "to process" with all its possible meanings as is done in the dictionary, the interpreter first thinks of *what* "processed cheese" is, *visualizes it* and finally says what kind of cheese it is in French.

Interpreting therefore also requires an ability to express oneself clearly, and an excellent command of one's native language and the way it is spoken in order to be able to express oneself appropriately in all situations.

Of course, the interpreter is not always familiar with all the expressions used in specialized fields. He may know or understand something perfectly without being able to immediately find the standard equivalent used by experts in the field. This is often the case when the expression is highly specialized. He nevertheless usually manages to express the meaning so clearly that the listener often feels he has heard the right word simply because he has understood the meaning.

The goal of the interpreter is to transmit the message with total accuracy, i.e., to have his listeners understand it as well as it was understood by those who heard it directly from the speaker himself. To accomplish this he must do more than understand the message in its entirety. Even the best analysis is worth nothing if it cannot afterwards be expressed in the appropriate words. Conference participants are scarcely aware of the process by which a speech is first understood and then re-expressed. To them it seems to involve nothing more than knowing the requisite terminology. They heartily congratulate the interpreter on his knowledge of the technical vocabulary, usually failing to notice that they were the ones who supplied him with most of it throughout the conference, and that it was his ability to understand and to express that enabled them to understand the semantic content of the message he was conveying to them.

Yet, however much we state that once a thought is completely understood it can be readily expressed, the fact that several working languages are used at the same international conference does affect the interpreter. Linguistic interference has become a fact of life. French newspapers, to take just one example, publish information that they have obtained from English-language wire services. Such news items are peppered with anglicisms, many of which find ready acceptance in French. The phenomenon also occurs in bilingual areas and with individuals who speak several languages. No one who is in contact with another language can totally escape it.

Linguistic interference is particularly apparent at international conferences. I remember hearing an eminent French businessman say, *Je vais vous* **introduire** *l'orateur*, instead of *introducing* the speaker with the words *Je vous présente l'orateur*. An equally distinguished professor from the Sorbonne once spoke of **le patron** *de développement juvénile*, when referring to "the pattern of juvenile development." In the same way I witnessed the English of a well-known American technical expert steadily deteriorate over the course of a few hours of dialogue with a French expert. The American very quickly abandoned the use of the correct term for the type of excavator he was speaking of ("reclaimer") and, upon hearing the French *gratteur*, he began to use the word "scraper"; what is more, when he heard the French word *sondages* being used, he stopped using "drilling" which he had used at the beginning of the discussion and began to use "sounding."

This phenomenon is the result of a normal desire to make oneself understood; speakers at conferences want to communicate, and in order to be understood, they adapt their expressions to those of the listeners. This does indeed bring the languages closer, but it distorts them at the same time. Conversely, this same desire for communication in a monolingual context produces a clarity that enriches the message being conveyed.

In consecutive interpretation the time lag involved makes it easier for the interpreter to forget the words of the speaker and, with them, the source language, and he thereby escapes, more or less naturally, the effects of linguistic contamination. In simultaneous, on the other hand, the interpreter is speaking while the language used by the speaker is constantly resounding in his ears. Here interference is much more of a problem, and although speaking and listening at the same time is not as difficult as the average person might think, it is decidedly difficult for the interpreter to refrain from repeating, simply by adjusting the pronunciation, words from the source language that are etymologically or phonetically related to words in his own language. He is tempted to translate the primary meaning of the word instead of the meaning it has in that context and has to make a conscious effort not to say "scraper" for *gratteur*, "sounding" for *sondages* or to come up with the word *hybridation* in French, when he has just heard "hybridization" in English.

For people who are not speaking through an intermediary, this linguistic contamination is a positive factor because communication is facilitated by such adaptation to one's listener. On the other hand, when this interference affects what the interpreter is saying, it causes confusion and misunderstanding. In this case the interference does not come from the language of the person to whom he is speaking but from the language of the speaker whom the interpreter is supposed to be translating for those who do not understand him. His role as a third party to a dialogue thus leads him to consciously resist interference from the language he hears and to do his utmost to deliberately adapt his own language to that of his listener.

While the young interpreter must consciously strive to resist linguistic interference, this effort becomes second nature to the experienced interpreter, to the extent that he will often choose not to use the easy equivalent of the word he hears in the source language, even when this would be perfectly correct; instead he chooses a word that is, phonologically and semantically, as different as possible from the original word.

The risks of interference are greater with languages that have a common origin. It is tempting to say *périlleux* for *pericoloso* and *mauvais garçons* for *malviventi* when interpreting from Italian to French, while it would be more correct and more reflective of the speaker's style (which is quite unpretentious) to say *dangereux* and *bandits* for these two terms. To a lesser degree English and French pose the same type of problem. Similar words in the two languages often do have similar meanings but there is the danger that they might belong to different registers or quite simply turn out to be "false friends."

However, although interference may in the case of closely related languages produce an interpretation that is mediocre, it is not likely to be completely unintelligible, since part of the message will get through despite the unusual turns of phrase. On the other hand, with languages that do not share similar grammatical or lexical structures, interference is less obvious but much more insidious because concepts are expressed in a very different manner and too literal a translation would produce a largely unintelligible interpretation (i.e., German or Japanese translated literally into French or English).

3. THE CREATIVITY OF EXPRESSION

In the process of conveying a message at high speed, discarding the original words but accurately rendering their meaning, the interpreter often comes up with words and expressions that, when compared to the original, are quite amazing. Upon examination, however, one realizes that words and expressions are in perfect harmony with the logic of the speech and are always chosen in the interests of clarity.

The following are some examples gleaned during a meeting where English and German were interpreted simultaneously into French. In the English sentence, "If anyone has a genius for managing money," "managing" was rendered by *faire fructifier*, which made the meaning much clearer than if *gérer* or *administrer* had been used. For the German sentence "*in diesem Entwicklungsland...wo sich die Regierung eine unbrauchbare Maschine hatte* **aufschwatzen** *lassen,*"[1] the interpreter produced "*... le gouvernement s'était fait* **embobiner**." Examined separately, these two terms (*aufschwatzen* and *embobiner*) have nothing in common, neither etymologically nor semantically. By giving it some thought, and by bearing in mind the meaning of the original word, the interpreter might have found another term that would have been closer to *aufschwatzen*, but *embobiner* did consummate justice to the German speaker. The meaning of his words was quite clear to his French-speaking listeners and the interpreter adhered to the colloquial style of the German by using a word that was just as colorful as the speaker's and just as idiomatic as the German.

The interpreter's job is not to render by a single word or phrase all the various meanings that a word may have in the source language, nor is it to translate one of those meanings out of context; rather, he must come up with the most appropriate words and phrases to convey the content and style of the message, regardless of the source language. At the same time he must make a constant effort to be clear and accurate, especially as he hears the speaker's

---

[1]English translation: "In this developing country ... where the Government has been conned into buying a useless piece of machinery."

message only once, states it only once, and thus has only one opportunity to make himself understood.

The interpreter is constantly striving to have his listener react to what the speaker says in the way the speaker intended. Let us make clear right here that we are not talking about "esthetic" language, the language the artist uses to commune with like-minded spirits. No, we are speaking here of "cybernetic" speech, which is the form an oral message assumes when it is directed toward a specific purpose that is achieved only when the listener reacts. This is quite obvious to the speaker who is addressing an audience in their own language — he will be understood only if dialogue ensues and if the listeners react to exactly "what" he said. The interpreter must have the same effect on those listening to him.

Let us consider one more example in this connection: that of the word "background," so common in English. In French, "background" can be *arrière-plan* or *toile de fond*, but when it is used in a conversation between two people seeking common points of interest, as in "What is your background?," a French-speaking interpreter does not hear "background" as having either of these meanings; rather, he thinks of the response that the speaker is trying to elicit from the listener and will thus say "*Quelle est votre formation?*" In the same way he would render "background paper" by *texte d'information générale*, or "against that background" by *dans le contexte* and would even use the word *origine* in rendering the phrases "immigrants with various backgrounds." He will choose widely different ways of expressing himself depending on the overall meaning of the statement, regardless of the dictionary definitions of "background."

In an earlier chapter we said that an interpreter is not a walking dictionary inasmuch as he cannot reel off the dozens of terms that might correspond to the English word "background" but that, depending on the context, he *devises* equivalents that most appropriately express the speaker's intent. This is how, in attempting to express as freely as possible what has become his own idea, he sometimes comes up with brilliant finds which would seem to be the result of studied preparation; yet it is simply his concern to make himself understood that gives his interpretation such an idiomatic flavor and enables him to convey the impact of the original statement. So, although the "foreign" listener does not hear the same words as the listener who hears the speech firsthand, he still hears the same thing.

Here is a relatively long excerpt taken from the consecutive interpretation of a speech. Talking about the war in Viet Nam an American speaker said:

The old emotional commitment has long since drowned in the hopeless swamps of the Delta. The China Lobby is ageing and enfeebled. The demand for a complete withdrawal becomes daily more vocal inside Congress and even within the Administration. The Americans would gladly pull out tomorrow if they could honestly persuade themselves that this would be the end of the story.

Here is the interpretation as it was recorded on tape:

L'ardeur qui les animait au début s'est enlisée depuis longtemps dans les marécages fétides du delta. Le lobby chinois est vieux et usé, son influence s'affaiblit de jour en jour. Des voix se font entendre de plus en plus fortes, au Congrès, parfois même au sein du gouvernement: "Que les Américains retirent leurs troupes!" Les Américains plieraient certainement volontiers bagages s'ils avaient la conviction que leur départ n'entraînerait pas de conséquences catastrophiques.

Although I have had twenty-five years of experience in the profession and although the purpose of this book is to show what interpretation is, I hesitated before including this example which is so typical of consecutive interpretation. Looking it over on paper I can imagine the traditional objections like "That's not what he *said*": "old emotional commitment" is not *une ardeur qui animait*, "hopeless" is not *fétide*, "tomorrow" is not *certainement*. But let us examine this text more closely. In order to reproduce the words of the consecutive interpretation on paper I have had to record them and in so doing, I have changed the nature of my example. By putting the spoken word down on paper I have robbed it of its evanescent character and laid it open to scrutiny. The reader of a text can ponder a word without the meaning of the rest of the sentence or idea getting irretrievably lost. In listening to a speech, however, one has to decide whether to concentrate on what is being said or to focus on one particular word at the risk of missing what follows. If

94

we look at the way in which we listen to any speech in our own language, we would find that we do not listen to the syntax of it – no one upon hearing this speech would have noticed that a swamp can hardly be "hopeless." What is more, the speaker probably did not choose these terms intentionally and was probably unaware that he had used them. Did the meaning of the word "hopeless" have special importance in and of itself or was it simply used to emphasize the overall tone of the statement by conjuring up a lot more than was explicitly referred to? The interpreter does not have time to ask himself these questions and yet he answers them when he automatically pairs *marécages* with an adjective that sounds correct in French. I would contend the word *fétide* in this example conjures up similar allusions to those of "hopeless" and that the overall tone of the sentence is successfully conveyed to French listeners by the use of a word pair that sounds familiar to them. While I do not claim that *fétide* is the translation of "hopeless," I do maintain that this interpretation, carried out in 30 seconds, conveyed the same message to the French-speaking listeners as the English-speaking listeners received in all its detail, with the same shades of meaning and in a comparable style. I would also maintain that the message was immediately comprehensible to the French-speaking listeners and, even though they were unable to remember the exact words used in French or English, both groups of listeners understood the same message in its entirety.

Perhaps a translator could come up with a better rendition of this passage if it were given to him as a written text. It might be written differently in French, but it would also be possible to restate the message differently in English.

The reason why I constantly emphasize that acts of speech are fleeting and that a passage of the length of the above excerpt has to be interpreted in a few seconds is not to make excuses for what might become a better translation if more time were taken over it, but to emphasize one of the steps in the rather astonishing process by which a message is rendered in another language at the speed of the spoken word.

4. COMMUNICATION AND PURITY OF LANGUAGE

Although the interpreter does his utmost to avoid the use of incorrect language and attempts to find the right terms which will help him achieve his goal (communication), he does not consider himself a purist. He is neither doggedly reactionary nor unduly innovative with respect to the use of vocabulary in his own language. He does not stick unrealistically to the "correct" meaning of a word that is on its way out; neither does he attempt to introduce new word meanings.

In fact, to the interpreter, language is not a static entity, but rather a means of communication which is constantly evolving in order to adapt to changing circumstances. He would be just as remiss in his duty if he resisted unduly the use of terms that were not genuinely French as he would be if he did not take care to avoid them when his listeners were unfamiliar with them. For example, although he is aware of the term *cadre* in French as it is used by movers, he will readily use the word *container* or *conteneur* rather than *cadre* with French railroad people or freight forwarders because he knows that the word *cadre*, with its older, more archaic connotation, might confuse those who are accustomed to speaking of *containers* or *conteneurs*. *The interpreter thus expresses himself in terms that the listener uses*, even if it sometimes means using "Franglais."

He knows that *standardisation* is an anglicism for the correct French term *normalisation*, but he is also aware of the pejorative connotation *standardisation* has taken on in French and so he will use it when he needs to express this particular shade of meaning. He knows that it is unnecessary to add the word *économique* after the word *conjoncture* when he hears *Konjunktur*[2] in a German speech on economics because French economists are accustomed to using this term by itself.

In the case of new and rapidly developing fields, the interpreter will take care to preserve foreign words for as long as an official French version has not been found. This is why for some time at least, he will use *chauffe* for "warm-up" and *jeu de rôle* for "role-playing" when talking about psychodrama; similarly, in electronics he

---

[2]"Economic situation," "business cycle," etc.

96

will not say *exploiter des renseignements*, but rather *traiter des données*, for "data processing."

The interpreter is aware that he is transmitting a message that will be short-lived and that, consequently, his sole responsibility is *to make sure that his listeners immediately understand what has been said*; to do this he must use terms with which they are familiar. Just as the grammarian Ferdinand Brunot noted the presence of an adverb "*ti*" when he heard the phrase *c'es**t-y**-là?*, the interpreter notes the presence of terms that he can use to bring about communication.

The interpreter is not a purist, but he is an orator in the classic sense of the word. He picks expressions that drive the message home, he speaks the language of his listeners, which means that he is also able to say *investissements* when necessary, even if the English word was "cost," and *service commercial* for "sales organization" when the context requires it; in another situation, he will come up with *compte rendu* and not *procès-verbal* for "minutes" and produce *comité de gérance* for a specific "board" rather than *conseil d'administration*.

Similarly, when an interpreter working into English realizes that his only listeners are Americans who do not understand specifically British English expressions, he will switch (however reluctantly) to their wavelength, and say "elevator" instead of "lift," "a couple of weeks" instead of a "fortnight," "truck" and "radio" instead of "lorry" and "wireless." He avoids aping Americanisms or making up artificial ones, but picks up, as he should, the expressions as they are used in context by his listeners.

On the other hand, the interpreter resists the linguistic interference caused by the presence of several languages in a meeting and avoids literal translations by turning the situation in which he works to his own advantage, relying on his listeners and using their language as a basis for modifying his own. He makes himself understood by sizing up the recipient of the message, just as he understood the message in the first place by sizing up the speaker. He adjusts his own language to suit his listeners and we shall see that the adjustment not only influences his choice of words, but also causes him to make his message more or less explicit depending on the amount of common ground the listener and the speaker share and on the purpose of each of their statements.

But before moving on to that subject, we must digress a moment and focus once again on the setting of an international conference.

5. THE INTERPRETER'S PRESENCE

Participants at international conferences would like to be able to communicate with one another directly as if they were all speaking the same language. Since they are used to this direct form of dialogue, they are sometimes bothered by the intervention of the interpreter. Like motorists who get irritated by the slowness of traffic crossing a bridge and who curse the bridge instead of the river, participants tend to forget that, while the interpreter enables them to move from one language to another and thus overcome the language barrier, he is not there to eliminate it completely. His task is to help participants understand each other's cultural differences rather than pretend that they do not exist.

The interpreter is an intermediary, like the actor whose style of acting complements the playwright's script. And like the actor, he knows that to put his message across successfully, he must not be self-effacing but, on the contrary, make his presence very much felt. Like the actor, the interpreter is good or not so good and, like him, his presence is always felt.

Although his role is different from that of the delegates at a meeting, the interpreter participates in it just as actively as they do. An international conference is thus a "trilogue," in which the interpreter seeks neither to emphasize his presence nor to play it down but simply to play his role. He realizes how much he contributes to the smooth running of the conference and knows where to draw the line between saying enough to do his job properly and establish communication between delegates, and saying anything that would run counter to his role or over-involve him in the dialogue to the point where he would color the message with his own ideas.

In this connection, I remember that one of my first jobs as a young interpreter was to accompany a group of French journalists to the pressroom of a large American newspaper. One of them asked me to enquire about the number of *sorties* the press had. I did not know what a *sortie* was, yet I needed to understand what the term meant in order to ask the question in English. When I asked the journalist what it meant, he simply told me to "translate it without trying to understand it." He undoubtedly felt that as an interpreter I was not there to learn and that I was probably taking advantage of the situation to improve my own knowledge. Yet my ignorance of the term *sortie* prevented the dialogue from continuing, so it was essential that I call attention to myself in order to be able to explain what a *sortie* was since I did not know the English equivalent (I learned in the process that it was a "folder").

Conscious of the task he must perform, the interpreter constantly strives to have the listeners understand what the speaker says, and to do this he speaks to them personally to "explain" to them what cannot be readily translated. Knowing that he must *transmit the meaning* of what he himself has understood, he does not hesitate to play his part in the trilogue. He will explain for instance that the speaker has made a joke or a play on words and render the essence of it if he cannot come up with a brilliant punchline on the spur of the moment. He will give a running commentary on the emerging elements of an idea whose full meaning only becomes clear to him several sentences later. In short, he cooperates with the listener to make sure he understands.

International conferences are here to stay and those who attend them are inevitably strangers to one another. To try and ignore the contribution of the interpreter would be tantamount to ignoring the international nature of conferences. There is no escaping him; he is the one who speaks to the audience in their own language, he is the one whose words they hear and whose presence they feel. The message that is ultimately transmitted to the foreign participant is the creation of two people, not one.

The interpreter who makes his presence felt and who stamps his interpretation with his own style, without of course omitting or changing anything said by the speaker, does not feel bound by the words of the original statement. By making full use of his analytical skills he knows just how far he should push an explanation and at what point he should exercise restraint and become as literal as possible.

Very little explanation is needed, for instance, when interpreting for officials of an international organization in their everyday work. Colleagues who are in daily contact have no problem understanding the purpose of the statements they exchange. They often acquire a working knowledge of the other language, and for them interpretation is frequently no more than an aid or a crutch which enables them to understand the finer points that they might otherwise have missed.

On the other hand, with delegates who come from very different cultures and who speak very different languages, the interpreter must sometimes be more explicit, concentrate on something that might otherwise have been misunderstood or explain something that was only alluded to. In no way, however, should this be taken to mean that he says anything different from the speaker because, as a party to the trilogue, he always refrains from assuming a delegate's role.

He also refrains from erasing all cultural differences; thus, he would not translate the Chinese word for "rice" by *pain* in French in an attempt to bridge the cultural gap that separates speaker from listener by trying to eliminate it. Interpreting an English speech into French *does not mean saying in French what a Frenchman would have said if he had been the speaker, but it does mean having the French-speaking listener understand what the English-speaking listener understood.*

The interpreter will therefore vary the amount of explanation he gives depending on how well the speaker and the listener know each other, but he will never try to hide the differences that separate them or underestimate their knowledge or intelligence. Translating a "mile" by "1.6 km" at a meeting of engineers would be ridiculous, and the interpreter who, during a meeting of Eastern and Western countries translated *democratie populaire* as used by a delegate from an Eastern European country by "communist regime" would indeed be misinterpreting the speaker. When it came to translating the American expression "rugged individualist," however, it would simply be for the sake of clarity if he were to explain that what was meant was not a non-conformist but someone who resists all government intervention and who is much more an advocate of free enterprise than he is an *individualiste* in the French sense of the term.

The degree of explanation involved in interpretation depends on the degree of mutual knowledge on the part of the speaker and the listener, the frequency or rarity of contact between their two cultures and their ability to understand one another, but the explanation itself is derived from nothing but the actual semantic content of the message. This means that the interpreter does not replace the speaker's idea with a different one; he will not say, for example as we have already shown, *pain* for "rice" if he is interpreting from Chinese to French.

In the last movement of his *Deutsches Requiem*, Brahms introduces trombones to signal the coming of the Last Judgment. He does so because in German religious texts it is trombones and not trumpets that announce the Last Judgment (*die Posaunen des Jüngsten Gerichtes*), so this instrument was chosen for good reason. The conductor of this Requiem in France or Britain would not substitute trumpets for trombones merely because the corresponding expressions in French and English refer to trumpets! He would no doubt prefer to explain in the program notes that Brahms chose trombones because the German biblical expression refers to trombones. The interpreter does exactly the same kind of thing!

6. STYLE

Although the interpreter uses his own words when he interprets, it is the *speaker's* ideas that he conveys and the *speaker's* style on which he models his own. He may very well resort to a paraphrase when the right word does not immediately occur to him and, like everyone else, he has his favorite expressions and turns of phrase. However, because the idea he receives is fully formed down to the last detail, he is able to identify the essential parts of the original form of the message, i.e., the images evoked and the type of words used.

A speaker's style is marked, among other things, by the basic choice he makes between rare or everyday words. The choice of one kind of word over another will make the difference between a lofty style and a colloquial one. The interpreter senses the overall tone of the speech and shifts into gear with the speaker. His role in the trilogue will not lead him to adopt a style that is different from the speaker's; in other words, he will not adopt a down-to-earth style if the speaker's is elegant or vice versa. He will also take care not to mix the lofty with the colloquial. Thus he would not say *hocher du chef* for "nodding your heads" any more than he would say "your missus" when he hears the President of the Federal Republic of Germany refer to the *hochverehrte Gattin* of a visiting monarch.

However odd it may seem, the interpreter must be as free with words in order to render style correctly as he has to be in order to convey their meaning. "Nod" does mean *hocher* but the style of the English chairman of a meeting who might say "I see you nodding

101

your heads" would not be rendered adequately if the interpreter were to say *Je vous vois hocher de la tête*, because *what* was said was *Je vois que vous êtes d'accord*, or *Vous faites signe que oui*. By understanding what the speaker is driving at, the interpreter manages to reproduce his style in a way that is almost unconscious and which sometimes even enables him to interpret the speaker's plays on words with amazing aplomb. I remember a British chairman presiding over a series of discussions in a spirited manner, who pointed to the brochures displayed at the back of the room, saying "They are there for *attention*, not *retention*." Aware that some brochures had previously disappeared, I quite spontaneously came out with "*Vous êtes priés de* **regarder** *et non pas de* **garder**."

7. ELOQUENCE

It is on the occasion of formal statements, like those delivered at formal dinners, at the opening of a conference, or to express thanks, that style is the most important, for if the interpreter is to move the audience, the eloquence of his presentation is just as important as the content of the message, if not more so.

The famous actor Garrick claimed that he could move an audience to tears or laughter while reciting the alphabet by changing the inflection of his voice. Without going that far, we would say that the interpreter who is engaged in oratory focuses most of his attention on expression, rather than on analyzing the content. He analyzes the kind of emotion the speaker seeks to elicit as well as the way he does it. He distinguishes the type of politeness that is normal courtesy from that which is obsequious, he notes the turns of phrase that indicate the degree of deference implied, etc.

The overriding goal of the interpreter in this type of situation is to move his audience by his oratory, to charm them by the incantatory power of words, to play on the magic of sounds that is so important in the spoken language. In this kind of interpretation the interpreter strives to reproduce the shades of meaning of each word as closely as possible. When rendering this type of discourse in consecutive, he jots down more adjectives and turns of phrase than on any other occasion and pays far more attention than otherwise to the expressions and form of the original. His performance thus draws on the full range of his oratorical skills. His jokes spark laughter, his flattery pleases, his audience is really moved, and the applause is genuine.

As always, the interpreter says exactly what the speaker says but he is mindful of the fact that, for once, he is addressing a passive audience and that it is preferable to skip over, for example, a reference to an argument between an Englishman and a Scotsman in a speech where the main focus is on something entirely different, rather than go into it in great detail and risk boring the French-speaking listeners.

On such occasions the interpreter does justice to the speaker by giving an eloquent interpretation, for his task is not to explain something to the listener or persuade him — but rather to move him.

CHAPTER V

INTERPRETING IN PRACTICE

In the preceding chapters we have attempted to describe what is involved in interpretation. We have seen that it cannot eliminate the language barrier, but that it does seek to overcome it, and in so doing, makes it possible for those listening to understand the original message.

We have also outlined the various stages in the process of interpretation. For that process to work satisfactorily at all, however, a certain number of essential conditions must first be met. We shall now turn our attention to these conditions. Where they are met, as in some large international organizations or in political and economic meetings of more limited scope (but at least as demanding in terms of interpreting skills), the process can function properly. Where they are not, interpretation cannot fulfill its potential. Unfortunately, this is all too often the case.

In all honesty, interpretation is often poor. Why? Well, sometimes the interpreter himself is bad, but more often the working conditions do not allow him to use his talents to the fullest. Of course, the quality of interpretation ranges all the way from the very fine to the totally useless and covers a broad spectrum between the absurdly literal and the perfect. We shall not attempt to describe all these variations in quality here, but we shall point out the problems that, if eliminated, would improve the quality of interpretation in general.

1. THE QUALITY OF THE INTERPRETER

First, it is quite evident that for interpretation to work, it must be performed by a qualified interpreter whose knowledge of languages is of the caliber we described earlier and who has received the kind of training that has developed his skills of analysis and comprehension as well as his powers of concentration and feeling for communication.[1] For a number of reasons, however, the requirements of the profession are not well known, and as a result it attracts many who are not qualified. There are many people with some knowledge of languages, but the notion of language competence is poorly defined; as to putting one language into another, it is usually seen simply as a matter of translating words. On the other hand, interpreting does not require expert knowledge in any field other than languages, and the profession is still too young for there to be any proper examination to control the flow of new entrants or any hard and fast regulations applicable to those who practice it.

The result is that the quality of interpretation is not always what it should be, particularly in simultaneous, where it is easier to do a poor job and get away with it. In *consecutive*, a bad interpreter will not last long because, whether they like it or not, the delegates hear his rendition into the other language. There are always some delegates present who know the target language sufficiently well to be able to judge the correctness of the interpretation, and the original speaker is a merciless judge of the consecutive interpreter. In *simultaneous*, on the other hand, those who understand the source language do not listen to the interpretation, and those who need to are not in a position to judge it on anything other than its coherence or intelligibility. They cannot challenge the correctness of the interpretation with specific examples and often cannot tell whether it was the speaker or the interpreter who was responsible for an incoherent or insipid statement. When they do criticize the interpretation they usually criticize it as a whole because they have neither the time nor the means to analyze in detail why it did not work nor, for that matter, any reason for doing so. Most of them therefore refrain from making specific criticisms of a service that is, after all, provided by the conference organizer. As a former director of the Ecole des Mines in Nancy once said, "I'm not one for complaining" while complaining, in private, about the quality of interpretation in a large European organization.

---

[1]At the ESIT School of Interpreters and Translators in Paris, Université Paris III — Sorbonne Nouvelle, the training course for conference interpreters lasts two years after the *licence* (first university degree).

This is not an isolated case, and it is easy to see why. Most participants do not realize that *good interpretation is possible* and that the first requirement is to *recruit qualified interpreters*. They tend to believe that the act of interpreting is too difficult to be performed well and excuse the interpreters. Perhaps they flatter their egos by thinking that the subjects they deal with are too difficult to interpret. For the most part, the only demand they make on the interpreter is that he give an approximate idea of the arguments being presented during a meeting. It is hardly surprising then that only interpreters who hesitate, get flustered or leave great gaps in their interpretation are eliminated while the cynical ones who skip what they do not understand and pad out their sentences with platitudes survive with little difficulty.

Moreover, if a multilingual participant were to look for evidence of the quality of simultaneous interpretation by checking up on specifics, he would have a very hard job on his hands. Many participants who are, by definition, unfamiliar with the problems involved in putting one language into another try to check the correctness of the translation by comparing individual words, losing sight of the meaning conveyed by both the original and the translation. They may thus grossly misjudge the quality of the interpretation. I am reminded of a Dutchman speaking on urban wastes in English while monitoring the French interpretation. The word "ashes" was quite correctly rendered by *mâchefer* but he did not know this term and was concerned at not hearing the word *cendres*. Even if he had known the correct French term and had congratulated the interpreter on the quality of his work, he would have been wrong to have based his judgment on the translation of a single word.

Only a professional interpreter can listen to two languages at the same time and accurately judge whether the *arguments* developed in the interpretation are the same as those of the original speech. Since he regularly shares a booth with his colleagues and hears both the original and the interpretation, the interpreter is able to compare them and can easily judge the quality of the interpretation. The delegates, on the other hand, can judge it solely on the basis of coherence and intelligibility. Until delegates become more demanding, a great deal of simultaneous will continue to be performed by inadequately qualified interpreters and the profession will continue to suffer from the lack of any legal protection.

At the present the only way of solving this problem would be to use much stricter selection and training procedures for would-be interpreters. We hope that the preceding chapters will help, by providing a better understanding of what is involved in interpretation.

However, even if one could always be sure of getting the right people, one would still not have created all the conditions necessary for proper interpretation; adverse circumstances can prevent even the best of interpreters from doing a first-rate job. Of course, it is the result that counts and if the interpretation is poor, it is practically impossible to tell whether it is because the sound system is second-rate or whether the interpreter is exhausted by too heavy a workload, or does not know the language well enough or is inadequately prepared to deal with the subject at hand, or if it is the speaker who is reading his text at a rate that makes it incomprehensible or the interpreter who does not understand it. Whatever the reasons, however, the result is clear: the interpretation is bad. For the purpose of this book, it seemed helpful to mention these different types of problems because we feel that it will be much easier to solve them if they can be dealt with separately.

First, we shall outline the problems that stem from the mode of interpretation being used.[2]

2. CONSECUTIVE INTERPRETATION IN PRACTICE

In consecutive interpretation the interpreter does not start speaking until the original speaker has stopped. He therefore has time to analyze the message as a whole, which makes it easier for him to understand its meaning. The fact that he is there in the room, and that the speaker has stopped talking before he begins, means that he speaks to his listeners face to face and he actually becomes the speaker. The attention that is focused on him makes it easier to adapt his language to his audience. By the expression on their faces he can see whether or not they have understood him, and when they

---

[2]See *Practical Guide for Users of Conference Interpreting Services* published by AIIC under the auspices of the Union of International Associations.

respond, it is often to him that they address their remarks – a sure sign that they have understood.

The only problems that sometimes arise are due to the physical set-up. The room may be too large or the interpreter may be given a seat from which he has trouble hearing the speakers. All he has to do in this case is to move, or to interrupt the speaker and ask him to repeat what he has just said.

The only case in which the technique of consecutive interpretation cannot be applied is when a written speech is being read out; but this is a problem that we shall discuss separately.

Apart from this, it is also true that when consecutive is used in a meeting with three working languages, the progress of the meeting suffers because of the repetition of the same speech in two languages. This repetition imposes a certain rigidity on the meeting, has a dampening effect on the proceedings and hampers the interpreter in his attempt to communicate with an audience that is only partially attentive. Some of the rapport between speaker and listener is lost because the dual rendering of the speech lends greater formality to the meeting and, since it would be awkward for the two interpreters working if they were to say slightly different things, their renditions become more literal, more rigid. As a consequence, the interpretation loses some of the spontaneity that it normally has when it is used in bilingual meetings where the interpreter can give full rein to his role as a participant in a trilogue. With the exception of formal occasions, it is probably preferable to use simultaneous for meetings with more than two working languages.

In bilingual meetings, it would be wrong to believe that consecutive interpretation will lengthen the meeting time. The number of words uttered by the speakers is obviously half of what it would be if simultaneous were being used or if there were no interpretation at all. However, the meeting time is always more or less predetermined and the type of interpretation used, or even its absence, does not significantly alter that. Furthermore, the number of words necessary to exhaust a certain subject is not a fixed quantity. The amount of information exchanged (or for that matter the quality of an agreement) does not depend on the number of words uttered, but rather on the caliber of the participants, their intelligence, their willingness to compromise, their capacity for understanding and so forth.

The thinking time that consecutive interpretation necessarily imposes on the participants at a meeting certainly helps to concentrate the discussions, and because of this we would argue that *consecutive interpretation actually saves time*. The participant who is prompted, by association of ideas, to relate an anecdote that the preceding speech reminded him of, decides against it during the interruption for consecutive interpretation; the delegates who speak language X have time to think while the interpretation is being done into language Y, and vice versa. Thus it is not the discussion time, but the thinking time that is doubled when the speaking time is cut by half. This finding is borne out whenever parallel meetings are held: those that use consecutive gain in conciseness and efficiency and progress much more quickly than those that use simultaneous or do not use interpretation at all.

3. SIMULTANEOUS INTERPRETATION IN PRACTICE

In simultaneous interpretation the interpreter is isolated in a booth. He speaks at the same time as the speaker and therefore has no need to memorize or jot down what is said. Moreover, the processes of analysis-comprehension and of reconstruction-expression are telescoped. The interpreter works on the message bit by bit, giving the portion he has understood while analyzing and assimilating the next idea.

The interpreter cannot wait for the speaker to develop his entire argument to understand the full implications of each sentence. In order to grasp the sense of what he hears, therefore, he has to compensate for the quicker pace at which the process of analysis-expression is to be carried out by drawing on a broader knowledge of the subject at hand. Thus there is a significant difference in the amount of knowledge needed by the simultaneous interpreter as compared to that of the consecutive interpreter to achieve equal performance.

Furthermore, in simultaneous, the interpreter's presence is not as conspicuous as it is in consecutive. Delegates listen to the interpretation through their earphones much as they might listen to the radio. They do not see the interpreter – in any case they do not look at him. Their eyes are fixed on the speaker who is speaking a language that is foreign to them and whose expressions and gestures become clear with a slight delay as the interpretation progresses. Unconsciously the listener expects the interpreter to perform as if he were reading a written translation. This is why the simultaneous interpreter must be able to manipulate the language with greater precision; he must possess a vocabulary that he can tap more readily in consecutive, as well as the ability to restructure language much more quickly. He must also make his own presence more clearly felt so as to be able to judge by the reactions of his listeners whether or not they are following and have understood what he is saying. The interpreter will, from time to time, step out of his anonymous role and speak to his listeners personally to make sure that they have understood, to alert them to problems he has run up against, or to advise them how to speak so that they will be understood in the other languages when it is their turn to address the meeting. In other words, he goes out of his way to establish the kind of rapport that occurs spontaneously in consecutive and which is essential to the smooth running of discussions between "foreigners."

Finally, one of the most difficult constraints imposed on an interpreter in simultaneous is that of not being able to work at his own speed. In consecutive he can increase or relax his concentration according to the density of the information being given. He can reflect on the preceding complex idea while jotting down the commonplace one that follows, or he can take time to analyze an obscure idea without noting all its details and as a result render it more concisely but also more coherently in his interpretation. In simultaneous, on the other hand, the speaker imposes his own speaking speed on the interpreter and yet they may not have the same type of mind or start from the same premises. The speaker reels off an idea that he has stated in much the same way at a host of previous meetings. The interpreter may find it surprising and incongruous and want to think about it, but he cannot, if he is to keep up with the speaker who has already passed on to his next point. The same holds true for the "translatable" words, some of which are part of the speaker's everyday vocabulary; for the interpreter, they require reflection when the equivalents do not immediately come to mind. The interpreter is thus caught up in a rhythm that is unnatural for him and which is a source of considerable fatigue — a subject we shall come back to later.

In concluding this comparison between consecutive and simultaneous interpretation in practice, let us simply state that, if equal results are to be obtained, both simultaneous and consecutive interpretation must be performed by equally qualified interpreters. Although one often hears people say that simultaneous is easier than consecutive, this is a mere illusion which only survives because bad interpreters themselves manage to survive in simultaneous. As we have just seen, it is difficult to prove that performance in simultaneous interpretation has been poor, whereas in consecutive the success or failure of the interpreter is immediately obvious.

What is easier about simultaneous, therefore, is not the actual mode of interpretation, but survival in the profession despite poor performance. To conclude from this that simultaneous is easier than consecutive would be quite unjustified. The fact that simultaneous is often not what it could or should be, is not, however, due solely to poor hiring standards. There are other reasons why the quality of interpretation is below par, even when it is being performed by the ablest of interpreters.

4. TECHNICAL WORKING CONDITIONS

Interpreting is unfortunately too young a profession for those who practice it to be able to do so under optimum conditions. The example of the technical conditions that complicate the task of the simultaneous interpreter, and at times makes it impossible, is very revealing in this respect.

An interpreter who cannot hear the speaker properly can be compared to someone in the top balcony of a theater who makes such an effort to hear the actor that he ceases to feel the impact of his words. What this person experiences is a type of auditory deficiency found in the hard-of-hearing, among whom three categories can be distinguished: (1) those who hear and understand, (2) *those who hear without understanding*, and (3) those who do not hear at all. The interpreter who is forced to work with equipment that is inadequate for the needs of interpretation finds himself in the second category. Forced to listen closely, his attention is automatically diverted away from the analysis of the meaning; his attempts to piece together the sounds that make up the words prevent him from perceiving the semantic relationship between them and cause him to lose parts of the meaning. The same principle applies to visual perception. When one is asked to decipher the sixth carbon copy of a typescript or a poorly written document in longhand, one's attention is initially focused on deciphering the individual words and a second reading is necessary to find out what the text means.

The amount of attention of which any one individual is capable is limited and is divided between perception of the form of a message and comprehension of its content. The more attention that is focused on perception the less there is available for comprehension, which means that the intellectual or emotional apprehension of the message depends on the ease with which it is perceived; instant comprehension occurs only if perception is effortless.

Interpretation suffers greatly when the full sound range does not come over. *The interpreter needs to hear without having to listen.* As soon as he has to make a conscious effort to perceive what is being said, his attention is diverted, his technique upset and he begins to give a literal translation instead of re-expressing the meaning of the message. He is no longer working up to par and the irritation he feels is a further source of interference which affects his concentration.

Unfortunately, not all manufacturers of interpreting equipment have yet recognized the need to produce a sound system that would enable the interpreter to understand without having to make an effort to listen. Some firms have done so, but others, including large companies famous the world over for their products in other areas, have shown little concern for the special needs of interpretation and provide equipment that leaves a lot to be desired. They seem to forget that the interpreter speaks and listens at the same time and that his voice should not drown out the voice of the speaker which he hears coming through his earphones; the sound volume must therefore be turned up high, *but without distorting the quality of the sound.* The fact is that the interpreter's *auditory perception* has a dual focus: the speaker's voice as well as his own, which is why the quality of the sound transmitted must be very good. On the other hand, the interpreter's earphones must not be covered with soundproof pads that prevent him from hearing his own voice. He needs to hear it to monitor the meaning of what he says while simultaneously and effortlessly hearing the speaker.

Memory, too, is to a certain extent dependent upon sound. We have seen that the interpreter stores the meaning of an idea while expressing the previous idea. There is a very short interval (at most a few seconds) between the time the speaker speaks and the time the interpreter starts on that part of the speech. Often, there are words (translatable terms, numbers, chemical formulae, proper names, etc.) that he must retain during this short interval without actively memorizing them or even attentively listening to them as any such distraction would seriously impede his analysis of the meaning. This is where memory span comes in, where auditory perception lingers on longer than it takes for the sounds to be emitted. Everyone knows that it is possible to count the chimes of a clock after it has stopped striking. For a very short time afterwards, it is possible to evoke the sounds and count up the chimes by "hearing" them again. It is as if man's auditory system contained a "recorder" which preserves sounds for a brief period before transferring them to the mind or erasing them. This faculty is of great importance in interpretation because, with sounds lingering on, the interpreter is able to recall them when he needs them a few seconds later. If the quality of the sound transmitted is poor, this advantage is completely lost and the interpreter is therefore forced to reduce the time lag between his words and those of the speaker, the meaning of the speech becomes less clear to him, the task more difficult, and he soon tires. Sound quality that is so poor that unconscious auditory recording cannot take place is thus a further cause of difficulty.

One last factor speaks in favor of very high standards in sound transmission, and that is *auditory reconstruction*. This reconstruction takes place unconsciously whenever sounds are partially lost in transmission. Over the telephone, for instance, a good many of the words heard are, in part, reconstructed. The sounds that reach the ear are sufficient to allow recognition of the words they represent without it being necessary for the listener to hear the entire word, although he has the impression that this is what he has in fact heard.

As soon as it comes to transmitting unfamiliar sounds, however, there is the problem of how much information is actually being transmitted. Take the simple example of dictating a telegram over the telephone. The operator has no difficulty taking down the text as long as it comprises only familiar words that can be expected in the context. But watch what happens when you give her a proper name. Not only will you have to spell it out letter by letter, but you will have to make sure that the letters themselves are not misunderstood by giving proper names or cities that begin with the same letters (e.g., "M as in Mary"). Similarly, someone speaking a foreign language is more difficult to understand over the telephone than face to face. The sounds conveyed are not as easy to recognize and make the task of reconstructing the total message much more difficult.

At international conferences many participants are unable to speak their native language because it is not one of the conference's working languages. A Nigerian or an Indian speaking English can be perfectly understandable face to face because there is no loss in transmission between the words leaving the mouth of the speaker and reaching the ear of the listener. Thus, after a bit of exposure, the listener can recognize the words in spite of their unfamiliar pronunciation. The situation is quite different, however, when those sounds are transmitted via electronic equipment with a narrow transmission band. Some of the sounds are lost altogether and those that do come through are often pronounced so atypically that they do not readily lend themselves to auditory reconstruction. As a result, simultaneous interpretation of a speech given in a language foreign to the speaker poses problems that would all but disappear if the quality of transmission were better.

Interpreters are often asked what they do whenever they hear, for example, a Japanese speak English in a manner that is totally incomprehensible. A number of anecdotes could be told in reply but actually this question is irrelevant. The interpreter is more accustomed to foreign accents than most of his listeners. He knows that Japanese tend to pronounce "l"s as "r"s and vice versa so that when he hears "plice" he knows it means "price," and, likewise, when he hears "prace" he knows it means "place." The interpreter also knows that the Dutch will often pronounce an "h" like "g" and vice versa. With good electronic equipment, and a good transmission band, most examples of this kind would not cause the interpreter any major difficulty. If the speaker really does have an inadequate command of the working languages of the conference, the interpreter can always request the documents from which the speaker will read and reconstruct the meaning from them. (It is unlikely that someone who does not speak a language well will speak without a text.) But the interpreter is no wizard; if the speech is totally incomprehensible, he has no recourse but to switch off his microphone. His listeners will be no worse off than those hearing the speaker firsthand. Neither will have understood the speech.

5. WRITTEN TEXTS

In the practice of the profession there are other obstacles that impede interpretation in the true sense of the word.

In conferences where delegates present their latest findings in a certain field and participate in the main to have the results of their research published, there is usually no dialogue but a series of monologues. The task that the interpreter is required to perform at such conferences is more akin to written translation than to interpretation. Under such circumstances there is a drop in the quality of interpretation and we shall see why.

The speaker who reads out his speech has spent days, if not weeks, drafting his paper. The expressions that he has set to paper are the result of a succession of mental processes which began with an intuitive intent and resulted in the final version read at the meeting. He has reread, corrected and revised his paper — yet he will take only about twenty minutes to deliver it orally. Papers presented at such congresses are not designed to elicit an immediate reaction from the listeners. They are also impervious to the context in which they are presented. Their authors are neither playwrights seeking a dramatic effect nor actors attempting to make a text come to life. They read their papers in a monotone, devoid of the rhythm and intonation that are part and parcel of the constant feedback between ideas and their formulation. During their delivery there are none of the pauses, changes of pace or repetitions which normally help to convey meaning and which give the spoken language its immediate intelligibility. Because the text is on paper, the speaker has no need to think about the content of his statement and, being spared the effort of formulating his thoughts, he does not slow down his delivery. A speech that is read out is delivered at a much more rapid pace than a statement made off the cuff (approximately 200 words per minute as opposed to 150 words per minute in extemporaneous speech); moreover, the density of information presented in a written text is generally greater.

116

Lacking spontaneity, the oral presentation of a written document is just as devoid of meaning as a play read by a non-actor in a monotone. When, at international conferences, speakers go up to the podium, one after the other, to deliver 15-minute papers that have no obvious relationship to each other, it becomes impossible even for experts to grasp the full meaning of the information presented. Experience shows that a written paper will not be discussed unless it has been submitted prior to the meeting and the listeners have been given a chance to digest the material before hearing it delivered.

Returning to the subject of the spoken language, it can be argued of course that not all those who speak off the cuff are great orators in the classic sense of the term. Even a poor speaker, however, is easier to understand than one who simply reads a paper. Speaking spontaneously actually requires performing three mental operations at the same time: thinking about the thoughts to be conveyed, expressing each idea aloud, and organizing and shaping the following thought on the basis of what has just been said. We have seen that this process produces about 9,000 words an hour.[3] However rapid this pace may seem, it represents the speed of mental processes connected with speaking and it is therefore suited to the understanding capabilities of listeners of comparable intelligence and background. An interpreter listening to a speaker speaking off the cuff is therefore in a good position to understand, since he can turn words into ideas at the same speed as the speaker turns ideas into words; he is thus able to keep up with the speaker's delivery. In terms of a written text, the spoken language is more like a rough draft. By definition, a written text is intended to be read, and can be read over and over again, whereas the spoken word is meant to be heard once and once only.

A hybrid form of the two (a written text read aloud or recited from memory) means that the paper being presented has only a minimal chance of being fully understood when delivered and even less of a chance of being properly interpreted. A comparison could

---

[3]We have chosen the *number of words translated per hour* simply as a convenient yardstick. Elsewhere, however, we have emphasized the unimportance of the individual word in interpretation.

117

be drawn between the time it takes to do a written translation, which is roughly equivalent to the time needed to write the original text, and the time it takes to interpret a speech, which is equivalent to the time needed to deliver it off the cuff. The United Nations has laid down six to eight pages of translation as the average amount of work that can be expected from its translators per day. This figure would seem to substantiate the hypothesis we have made concerning the relationship between the amount of time needed for drafting and that needed for translating.

Interpreters are often called on to do "on-sight" translations, i.e., to give an on-the-spot oral rendering of a written text as it is being read out at the meetings. This amounts to asking them to convey messages which, because of their form and the way in which they are presented, are not amenable to interpretation at all and this at a speed of 200 words per minute, or 40 times faster than normal translating work. This absurd pace quickly reduces the interpreter to a state of mental and physical exhaustion, and his usefulness to the listener is practically nil, when compared to the service he is able to render when dealing with a free speech. Placed in an impossible situation, he gives up trying to understand: he leaves his sentences unfinished, becomes breathless and frustrated, soothes his troubled conscience when he sees that his colleagues are managing no better than he, is happy to translate a word or two correctly here and there, curses the day he accepted that particular conference, leaves the booth as soon as the meeting is over and vanishes gratefully into the anonymity of the crowd. The best interpreters, however, those who have proved themselves worthy of the name, refuse to jeopardize their profession's reputation by working under these impossible conditions. They simply switch off their microphones.

The only possible solution to this serious problem is to give the interpreter the opportunity of thoroughly reviewing the documents that are to be delivered at a conference. He should be given a few days before the start of the conference to study and annotate the papers that he will be required to translate orally. In addition, a sufficient number of interpreters would have to be hired to staff the conference so that each one would have enough time, while his colleagues were at work in the booth, to go over the papers that come in at the last minute. This would mean that interpreters would be hired for a longer period of time, the number of days of paid preparation being equal to the number of working days of the conference; it would also mean doubling or tripling the size of the interpretation teams.

6. THE LANGUAGE OF EXPRESSION

While it is essential that the interpreter receive the message under conditions that are favorable to good comprehension and analysis — which means that he should not find himself confronted with a written text or unable to hear the speaker for one reason or another — it is equally important that he be able to relay the message under conditions conducive to good expression. The market itself can sometimes be an obstacle to this. Some language combinations are all too rare. The number of native English-speaking interpreters who can interpret from French or German, for example, is not always sufficient to meet the market demand in Europe. This paucity of native English-speaking interpreters is coupled with a plethora of interpreters whose native languages are either French or German, so it not unusual to find French or German interpreters working in the English booth.

At present, therefore, simultaneous is often being performed under conditions that prevent it from *realizing its full potential*. We would contend that if one were to take two equally competent interpreters and have one work into his "A" (native) language and the other into his "B" (non-native) language, the end result would always be better from the "A" booth than from the "B" booth.

Let us take an interpreter whose native language is French, for example, and have him work first into French and then into English. Whether he is working in the French or English booth, his knowledge of the two languages does not change and neither does his knowledge of the subject matter, his intelligence, his analytical skill or capacity for comprehension. What does change — and quite markedly — is the quality of his expression, according to whether he is working into his native French or into English. It should be borne in mind that he has to restructure source-language expressions at the speed of the spoken word; hence what I have in mind when I say that an interpreter who works into his second language does not perform as well as when he is working into his native language is not a concern for grammaticality but a concern for communication.

Proper communication can come about only if all the links in the chain are there. The message must reach the listener as smoothly through the interpreter as it would if he were to hear it directly from the speaker. It is not enough for the interpreter to merely understand the message and transmit it in its entirety; he must also *formulate it in such a way that it reaches its target.* The interpreter working from his native into his non-native language has no difficulty understanding the language he hears: here, the line of communication between speaker and interpreter is smooth. However, the same does not apply to the line of communication between the interpreter and his listener. The interference of the native language on the second language is much stronger than the interference of the second language on the native language. What an interpreter lacks in his "B" language is the deeply rooted intuition for the language, the natural ease of expression necessary to restructure the form. When interpreting into his "B" language, the interpreter simply does not have the time to be the exegete he is in his "A" language where, in adapting his language to his listeners, he explains the message to them more than he translates it. In his non-native language it is difficult for him to bridge the gap between himself and his listeners. He knows what the message means, but the intelligibility of his wording suffers because he is limited in the ways in which he can express himself, and the listener who does not always understand fully what is being said sometimes wonders whether the language he is being offered is really his own.

Let us consider the example of a French-speaking listener who hears the words *faute d'esthétique* in the interpretation of a German speech into French. In using this particular term, the interpreter would be translating the primary meaning of the German *Schönheits-fehler*, yet the listener would not have understood it as well or as quickly as if he had heard the French word *imperfection*. In this situation, the listener would have to make an extra effort to fit this unusual expression into the context, and because it is unusual it would draw attention to itself and would thus acquire an importance that it did not have in the original statement. The fact that this expression would require more reflection on the part of the listener would prevent him from hearing the speaker's next point, thereby impairing his overall comprehension.

This is why we feel interpretation done into a "B" language is, necessarily, inferior to that done into an "A" language. Young interpreters at the start of their careers often prefer to work into their second language, which they feel is an easier task. Afraid of misunderstanding the foreign language, they prefer to speak it, without realizing how often what they say is unintelligible. Having managed to express themselves, they think that they have made themselves understood.

Beginners who believe that it is easier to work into their second language tend to forget that interpretation does not end with the interpreter understanding the message — it is not complete until the total message has reached the listener. They also forget that, although it is relatively easy to make oneself understood in another language when expressing one's own ideas at one's own speed, it is quite a different matter in interpretation where the constraints imposed by somebody else's thoughts require a much greater command of the language.

Interpreting into a "B" language in simultaneous is all the more regrettable as continued study will make it perfectly possible for an interpreter to acquire a very thorough knowledge of a foreign language to the point that he can be *certain of understanding it.* On the other hand, it is impossible, after a certain age, to learn to speak a foreign language perfectly. So that, all other things being equal, interpretation done into a "B" language is always less satisfactorily done than into an "A" language.

We should add, however, that interpreting into an "A" language is not a necessary requirement for all types of meetings. It is indispensable for oratory, but not as necessary for a descriptive statement, for example. When working into their second languages, professional interpreters choose their conferences very carefully. They pick conferences of a technical nature where translatable words abound and where a more literal approach is possible; they choose conferences where the participants have long-standing relationships with one another and where explanation is unnecessary. Or they will choose to use their "B" language for consecutive interpretation, as interference from one's native language is not as strong here as it is in simultaneous.

7. THE WORK LOAD

In an era of space exploration, interplanetary rockets and rendezvous in space, work is still judged in terms of time spent rather than effort expended. And yet, is it right for the person who works at his own pace and the one who works at a pace that is imposed on him to be required to put in the same number of hours? Should the switchboard operator, who works at a varying and imposed pace, be required to stay on the job as long as an office worker? Can the person who does physical labor expend his energy for as long as someone whose work is intellectual in nature? As a matter of interest, how does the work load of the interpreter compare with the conventional length of a working day?

Speaking Time

At international conferences, the meeting time — and hence an interpreter's working day — averages about six hours. Of these six hours, the interpreter is speaking about one-third of the time, since interpreters usually work in pairs in the booth. During the remainder of the time, the other interpreter speaks or, when the language of the booth is being spoken on the floor, the booth is silent. Given the speed of the spoken language, one hour of simultaneous interpretation amounts to approximately 9,000 words. In about two hours, therefore, an interpreter will have processed and uttered roughly 20,000 words. It is interesting to compare this figure of 20,000 words with the amount handled in written translation. As we saw earlier, the United Nations lays down a standard of between 6 and 8 pages, or 2,000 to 3,000 words per day. The daily contractual work load for conference translators is calculated on the basis of two thousand words for ordinary texts and one thousand words for technical texts. Thus, in one day, the interpreter processes *ten times as many words as the translator*. However, as these words are concentrated into the time the interpreter is actually speaking (one-third of the meeting time), the interpreter is in fact *working thirty times faster than a translator*. Whatever the fundamental differences between translation and interpretation, it is obvious that a working speed 3,000% greater than that of a translator cannot be sustained for long, which is why simultaneous interpreters relieve one another every 20 minutes or half hour.

Apart from the amount of "active" work that the interpreter does, and the speed with which he must accomplish it, there is the additional fatigue caused by the pace imposed on him. He cannot vary the rate of his delivery within the total framework of the speech, slowing down so as to be able to give more thought to certain complex passages and then speeding up again when he comes to simpler ones.

This pace, which is at odds with the effort being made, is a source of considerable fatigue. Moreover, by the time the interpreter has become accustomed to the style of one speaker, another one has taken his place and the interpreter finds himself forced to adapt to a new pace, a new style and a new way of expressing ideas. He cannot therefore rely on the type of conditioned reflexes that, for example, a worker on an assembly line acquires. Neither can he proceed in the same way as the translator, who can interrupt his work and who can also arrange his documents so that he can deal with the most difficult ones first thing in the morning after a good night's rest or, conversely, begin with the easiest text so that he can get off to a good start. Furthermore, the interpreter cannot give free rein to his own thoughts or interrupt his work to pick up the phone and make an appointment with his dentist. While he is absorbed in his work, hooked up to his microphone and earphones, the outside world ceases to exist.

Having thus described the intense effort involved in carrying out the interpreter's only visible job – speaking – we shall now briefly turn to two other aspects of his work which are carried out behind the scenes: listening and preparation.

Listening Time

When he is not actually speaking, the interpreter must spend time on another important part of his work: following the discussions. We have constantly stressed that the reason interpretation works at all is because the interpreter is there on the spot, able to take stock of the context, as well as of the person speaking and of the listener to whom his language is tailored. He must therefore listen when a delegate of his own language takes the floor not only to note down the words and expressions used but also, and above all, to follow the discussions and be ready to step into the "trilogue" when the time comes. He continues this monitoring process even after his colleague has taken over from him in the booth. This type of listening requires an effort from the interpreter that is similar in intensity to that required of delegates listening with a view to participating in the discussion.

Preparation Time

We have seen that, regardless of the interpreter's general knowledge, he should acquire for each conference (without of course trying to become as knowledgeable as the speaker in his own field) sufficient extra knowledge and vocabulary to enable him to understand and re-express the statements he will hear. Preparation should not be limited to conferences dealing with technical subjects, because, given the speaker's long years of work in his field, he will always be more knowledgeable than the interpreter about the subject at hand. Consequently there are *no* conferences for which the interpreter does not need to prepare.

It is difficult to estimate the amount of time involved in preparation. An interpreter prepares both before a meeting and also during the meeting. We could say that preparation time is more or less equivalent to speaking time, in other words about two or three hours per working day.

8. FATIGUE

If we were to add up the number of working hours involved in a day of simultaneous interpretation, we would thus find that productive work accounts for two or three hours a day, or 20,000 words of message, and that listening, just as exacting and responsible a task and as tiring for the interpreter as it is for the participants at a meeting, accounts for three to four additional hours. Finally, there is the preparation which conscientious interpreters do the night before, or even a few days before, by studying the working documents of the meeting.

If one considers, on top of this, that booths[4] have often been designed on the assumption that the interpreter will spend very little time there when in fact he spends entire days there; that they are, for the most part, poorly ventilated, uncomfortable and difficult to get out of for a breath of fresh air; that the interpreter's earphones are often of poor quality, which means the sound must be turned up so high that it causes headaches and acoustic traumas, it is hardly surprising that simultaneous interpretation often yields poor results. It is hardly surprising, either, that most interpreters seek to recuperate as best as they can, leave the booth when they are not working instead of following the discussions, fail to prepare sufficiently, and when fatigue sets in, as is inevitable after the meeting has been in progress for a couple of hours, give up trying to understand altogether, and from then on mechanically recite words that are suggested to them by those they hear in the other language, or even refuse straight out to try and understand (a very understandable tactic of self-preservation).

We will not improve this state of affairs by moral exhortation; no human being is capable of maintaining over a long period of time the effort that good simultaneous interpretation requires. The problem will be solved only when satisfactory working conditions have been established. This means, first and foremost, significantly increasing the number of interpreters hired for a conference and therefore reducing the working time of each interpreter by at least a half. It would follow thus that, at the very least, the number of interpreters would at least be doubled, that a much greater part of the individual interpreter's working day would be devoted to preparation and listening, and that the amount of speaking time would be reduced proportionately.

---

[4]Since this book was first published in 1968, considerable improvements have been made to booth and sound system specifications, thanks particularly to the adoption of ISO Standard 2603-1974, "Booths for simultaneous interpretation. General characteristics and equipment."

In this way, interpretation could be performed in a manner more consistent with the enormous effort it requires. It would take its place alongside professions that have been recognized as having a certain element of "performance," but an even larger "behind the scenes" side. No one expects teachers, for instance, to be in the classroom 40 hours a week or pianists to give six- or seven-hour concerts every day.

Yet, with interpretation, is should be noted that the enormous mental effort that the interpreter makes, coupled with the cramped and poorly ventilated surrounding in which he works, are a source of *fatigue*, the long-term consequences of which are bound to make themselves felt sooner or later.

To produce, within a period of time more suited to much less intensive mental activity, a quantity of work that is ten times greater than that of a translator, at a speed that is by necessity 30 times faster, imposes a strain which leads either to serious psychosomatic disorders or, as we said earlier, causes interpreters to shirk their responsibilities and do a bad job.

Modern medical research has established that one can maintain an efficient level of output for no more than 30 minutes at a time on a job that demands close attention and that cannot be performed by conditioned reflexes. This efficient level of output can be maintained for an hour and a quarter on a more repetitive job destined eventually to be performed by machines. Thirty minutes is roughly the amount of time that an interpreter works at a stretch. During this time he processes 4,500 words. Clearly he should have considerable time to recuperate before beginning to work again. For an interpreter to be able to do a good job, his working day would have to be divided into four parts. For every hour of actual speaking time he would devote about three hours to preparation, two to recuperation and one to listening. There's still a long way to go ....

CONCLUSION

Throughout this book we have tried to explain what interpretation is, what it can be under the best of circumstances, and what it always should be. We felt it necessary to do so because we have often noticed that, when placed in the right conditions, interpreters can achieve astonishing results which inspire respect and admiration, given the many and complex factors with which they must cope. But we have also seen that the conditions necessary for the interpreter to use his talents to the full are often lacking. The interpreter is acutely aware of the role he plays in the trilogue that takes place at international conferences but, because of circumstances beyond his control, he all too often finds himself in the position of a surgeon who must perform an operation with a simple kitchen knife.

In addition to the fact that professional interpreters are often forced to work under unreasonable working conditions which prevent them from giving of their best, the profession as such enjoys no legal protection whatsoever. Anybody who so wishes can call himself an interpreter and work at international conferences. As long as this situation prevails, the profession will never attain maturity and only partially fulfill its promise.

This is why we thought it essential to define the techniques and conditions that make conference interpreting work. This attempt is based on two score and some years of practice and teaching.

We have continually stressed that interpretation cannot be a word-for-word translation, and if at present there are still interpreters who try to use this technique, it is only because the languages they work with — English, French and Italian for instance — are closely related. Because many words look alike and have roughly the same meaning, the temptation is to proceed by analogy — and the end product is a bad translation. But the time will come when international exchanges between countries lying far apart will require more frequent use of interpretation. When it comes to interpreting French into Chinese or Japanese into English, for example, the analogy technique will be inapplicable simply because these languages are totally dissimilar. If interpretation is to work at all in such cases, the techniques we have described in this book will be absolutely essential.

It may, of course, be possible to approach the study of interpretation from other angles. A great deal of scientific research and painstaking analysis will have to be done, especially on the relationship between thought and language, before a comprehensive theory can be established. The interpreter, at the crossroads of two disciplines, is certainly an excellent guinea pig – what better way of testing theories of language and communication than by observing the interpreter at work?[5] Given the current state of our knowledge, a study such as this is bound to be of some interest, and we felt in any case that there was an urgent need to attempt a theory of interpretation at a time when the profession is no longer the domain of a few outstanding men and women but is coming to be accepted as part and parcel of our modern world.

Interpretation is currently passing through a phase where individual brilliance is of waning importance but where the reputation of the profession as a whole has not yet been firmly established. It has displayed abundant evidence of its potential, but because it has not been sufficiently studied or defined, it is not always in a position to realize that potential today. It had proved to be essential to our modern world, but its mode of practice has not yet found a firm theoretical basis. The more that is known about interpretation, the way it works and the possibilities it can offer, the greater will be its service to the modern world – service that the world expects from it and that it is perfectly capable of providing.

---

[5]Since this book was first published in French, such studies have been conducted. See:

D. Seleskovitch: *Langage, langues et mémoire, Etude de la prise de notes en interprétation consécutive*, Paris, Minard, Lettres Modernes, 1975.

M. Lederer: *La traduction simultanée, Fondements théoriques*, Paris, Minard, Lettres Modernes, 1981.

ANNEX I

Examples of the Variety of Subjects that a Professional Interpreter may be Called Upon to Handle

Conferences utilizing interpreters deal with ma. y diverse subjects. The vast range of human activities and the con_tant expansion of knowledge in each area have made exchanges of information more and more necessary and frequent. Rare is the field of activity nowadays, be it science or technology, finance or trade, agriculture or industry, arbitration tribunal or locust control, which does not extend beyond national borders, and thus involve more than one language.

Hence interpretation is no longer, as it once was, restricted to diplomatic exchanges, and the interpreter may be called upon, depending on his assignments, to work in each and every area of contemporary human activity. Here, by way of example, is a list of the subjects involved in recent interpretation assignments.

Assignments of a Washington, D.C.-based interpreter in a twelve-month period, 1993-94:

Sheet Metal
Boxing Match (TV)
NATO Defense Policy
Foreign Aid Policy
Science Policy
G-7 Summit
Banking Regulation
Concrete Masonry
IMF/World Bank Policies
Niche Software
Investment Banking
Interoperability of NATO Command and Control Equipment
Copyright Societies
Product Liability Lawsuit
Bilateral Social Security Agreement
Timeshare Real Estate

Election Night Broadcast (TV)
Materials Flow Management
Trucking
Health Care Systems
Hosiery Manufacturing
Credit Unions
Intermodal Transportation
OECD Seed Schemes
Insurance and Reinsurance
Foot Orthotics
Dentistry

* * * * *

One European interpreter's assignments for Austrian Television in 1993 (live interpretation from English into German):

Topics of Special Broadcasts:

U.S.-Iraq relations
Problems in the former Yugoslavia
Fifty years after the battle of Stalingrad
South Africa
Zbigniew Brezinski, lecture on the New World Order
Peace in the Middle East
The situation in Moscow
Nobel Peace Prize (Nelson Mandela and Willem de Klerk)
Round Table discussion on Austria and the European Union
World Conference on Human Rights (five broadcasts)
President Clinton's inauguration speech
President Clinton's State of the Union address
Vancouver Summit
Prince Philip speaking on the World Wildlife Fund

Interviews:

Haris Silajdzic, Bosnian Prime Minister
Yasser Arafat
Harry Belafonte

U.S. author Camille Paglia
Adviser to President Clinton
UNPROFOR representative (on Yugoslavia)
President Berisha of Albania
U.N. Secretary-General Boutros-Ghali

Talk show (featuring LaToya Jackson)
Several sports programs (covering a wide range of sports).

* * * * *

A Swiss free-lance interpreter covered the following subjects in 1993:

01/16-19	Creativity Research
01/20	Economic Survey Meeting
01/22	TV-interview with U.S. Economist (live)
01/27-28	FDA-Registration Policy
01/29	Motor Car Distributor Meeting
02/05	Freight Forwarding
02/16	Retailing
02/18	Solar Vehicle Show
02/25-27	Palliative Cancer Therapy
03/04	Direct Marketing
03/09-10	Electronic Imaging
03/11	Annual Press Conference of Transnational Heavy Engineering Group
03/12	Wound Care
03/15	Junior Management Training Seminar (Banking)
03/16-18	Telecommunications Group Management Seminar
03/19	Junior Management Training Seminar (Banking)
03/22-25	Mail Order Congress
03/26	Sales Promotion Meeting (Sunglasses)
03/27	Script Writing Seminar with U.S. Scriptwriter
03/29-30	Electronic Discharge Technology
04/03	International Judo Conference
04/14-16	Council of Europe Mission
04/18	Direct Marketing

04/19	Tourism
04/20	Epilepsy
04/21	Annual General Meeting of Multinational Corporation
04/22-23	Management Seminar of Multinational Kitchen Systems Group
04/24	Freight Forwarding
04/29	Electronic Data Interchange
05/05	Annual Press Conference of Multinational Telecommunications Group
05/13	Newspaper Design and Layout Seminar
05/14	Office Furniture Fair
05/17	Annual Press Conference of Swiss Heavy Engineering Group
05/25-26	Insurance Management Seminar
05/27	Annual General Meeting of Swiss Textile Group
06/02-04	Insurance Management Seminar
06/11-15	TV Technology Symposium
06/16-18	Computer User Group Meeting
06/23-25	Concrete Technology Symposium
06/28-	
07/02	Fluid Control Systems Seminar
08/10	Board Meeting of General Contracting Group
08/25-26	Bank Management Seminar
09/01-03	Environmental Risk Insurance Symposium
09/08	Food Distributor Press Conference
09/09	Annual General Meeting of Multinational Finance Corporation
09/10-11	Dental Technology
09/13-15	Board Meeting of Multinational Concrete Group
09/27-30	International Detergents Symposium
10/05	TV Sales Promotion Meeting
10/06	TV-interview with U.S. Rock Star (live)
10/07	Export Financing
10/15	Development Aid Seminar
10/20-22	Fundraising Workshop
10/25-27	Multinational Elevator Group Management Seminar
11/04-05	Accounting Seminar of German Multinational Group
11/16	Retailing
11/18	Food Services & Catering Industry Congress

11/19	Banking Symposium
11/26	Motor Car Distributor Meeting
11/30	Hotel Chain Management Meeting
12/01	Chemical Industry Meeting
12/09-10	Human Resources Management Seminar

* * * * *

These three lists clearly show the diversity of subjects which the interpreter must deal with.

ANNEX II

OTHER WORKS BY THE AUTHOR

Langage, Langues et Mémoire. Etude de la prise de notes en interprétation consécutive. Paris, Minard, 1975.

"Exégèse et Traduction." *Etudes de Linguistique Appliquée No. 12.* Paris, Didier, 1973.

"Zur Theorie des Dolmetschens," in KAPP, V. (ed.) *Übersetzer und Dolmetscher.* Heidelberg, Quelle & Meyer, 1974.

"Interpretation, a Psychological Approach to Translation," in BRISLIN, R. (ed.) *Translation: Applications and Research.* New York, Gardner Press, 1976.

"Traduire: les Idées et les Mots." *Etudes de Linguistique Appliquée No. 24.* Paris, Didier, 1976.

"Why Interpreting is not Tantamount to Translating Languages" (Threlford Memorial Lecture 1977). *The Incorporated Linguist*, Vol. 16, No. 2, London, 1977.

Pédagogie Raisonnée de l'Interprétation (co-authored with Marianne Lederer). Collection "Traductologie" No. 4. Paris: Didier Erudition, OPOCE, 1989.

INDEX